PRAISE FOR *SANT'ONOFRIO*

John Paul Sonnen guides his readers through a gripping tour of the church and cloister of Sant'Onofrio al Gianicolo: commencing with the life of the church's titular saint, the hermit Onuphrius, hidden in the desert of fourth-century Egypt; then to the edifice's appearance on the Janiculum Hill in Renaissance Rome — sheltering personages such as the great Italian poet Torquato Tasso (1544–1595) and the second apostle of Rome, St. Philip Neri (1515–1595); and concluding with a detailed excursion through the entire complex of Sant'Onofrio, which at present is the official church in Rome of the Equestrian Order of the Holy Sepulchre of Jerusalem. This fascinating tour is Catholic in its spirit and catholic in its wide embrace of the historical, geographical, and cultural dimensions of this Citadel of Faith.

— HIEROMONK GREGORY HRYNKIW, S.T.D., Hermitage of the Three Holy Hierarchs, author of *Cajetan on Sacred Doctrine* (CUA Press, 2020)

Mr. Sonnen's book offers an insightful and well-researched manual for this hidden gem in the heart of Rome. The reader will discover the noteworthy spiritual impact of the church and monastery in Rome through its link between Eastern and Western monasticism and such illustrious personages as St. Philip Neri. The self-guided tour offered in this volume makes it an indispensable companion for those already in love with the history and art of Sant'Onofrio or those who are setting out to discover it.

— DR. PHIL. JAN C. BENTZ, Professor for Philosophy of Art, The Catholic University of America, *Rome Campus*

This book will capture the hearts of members of the Knights and Dames of the Holy Sepulchre of

Jerusalem, Church historians, pilgrims who love the Eternal City and many others who love our Catholic Faith. In this book, John Paul Sonnen has artistically blended the history of the life of Saint Onuphrius, the grandeur and rich history of the Church of Sant'Onofrio al Giancolo and how this Church came to serve as the spiritual center to the Order of the Holy Sepulchre of Jerusalem in the city of Rome. I recommend this book to Knights and Dames of the Holy Sepulchre of Jerusalem and to anyone who loves the Eternal City, the seat of our Catholic Faith.

—FR. RANDAL KASEL, KHS, Chaplain of the Equestrian Order, Archdiocese of St. Paul and Minneapolis

St. Philip Neri used to hold outdoor religious exercises at Sant'Onofrio on the Janiculum Hill. It never occurred to me to ask who Sant'Onofrio was. The first biography of St. Philip that I read, by a learned 19th-century Italian Cardinal, connected St Philip and Sant'Onofrio with Tasso and Tasso's oak. His assurance that his readers would know who Tasso was made me too embarrassed to admit to myself that I didn't. John Paul Sonnen's book answers all the questions I failed to ask, and more. On my next trip to Rome, I intend to visit that beautiful spot with this book in hand as a guide.

—FR. DANIEL UTRECHT, Ph.D., The Toronto Oratory, author of *The Lion of Münster: The Bishop Who Roared Against the Nazis*

Often that which is most precious is hidden and discovered by Providence. This is true of the gem of the Church of Sant'Onofrio al Gianicolo in Rome described with an obvious devotion and reverence by John Paul Sonnen in his work bearing the subtitle "Journeying to a Citadel of Faith." Although hidden from the eyes of so many pilgrims and unknown even to many Romans, the Church is rich in history and a uniquely beautiful mixture of Renaissance and Baroque architecture.

In this brief work, Sonnen captures the impact that this Church had on the hearts and minds of so many people over the centuries; from the great poet Tasso to the second Apostle of Rome, Saint Philip Neri.

It was a refuge of prayer, contemplation and of joyful companionship for those who shared the faith and made it their destination of choice. Sonnen's love for Sant'Onofrio and its history invites the reader to "come and see."

St. Philip Neri in his holy genius made it the site of the new evangelization of the people of his day. As an Oratorian, therefore, I know now the first place I shall search out in haste on my next pilgrimage to the Holy City!

—**FR. DAVID SLOAN ABERNETHY**, C.O., The Pittsburgh Oratory, administrator of *Philokalia Ministries*

Sant'Onofrio al Gianicolo

Sant'Onofrio al Gianicolo

JOURNEYING TO A CITADEL OF FAITH

BY
JOHN PAUL SONNEN, KHS

Foreword by
Fr. Dana Ambrose Christensen, KHS

Copyright © Arouca Press 2021
Copyright © John Sonnen
Foreword © Dana Christensen

All rights reserved:
No part of this book may be reproduced or transmitted,
in any form or by any means, without permission

ISBN: 978-1-989905-68-5 (pbk)
ISBN: 978-1-989905-69-2 (hardcover)

Arouca Press
PO Box 55003
Bridgeport PO
Waterloo, ON N2J 3G0
Canada
www.aroucapress.com
Send inquiries to info@aroucapress.com

Cover image: *Blick vom Kloster Sant' Onofrio auf Rom* (View from Sant'Onofrio on Rome) (1835) by Rudolf von Alt, used with permission by the Leopold Museum, Vienna.
Excerpts have been taken from *Histories of the Monks of Upper Egypt and The Life of Onnophrius by Paphnutius with a Discourse on Saint Onnophrius by Pisentius of Coptos*, translated by Tim Vivian, used with permission, Copyright 2000 by Cistercian Publications, Inc. © 2008 by Order of Saint Benedict, Collegeville, Minn. Used with permission.
Except as indicated, all photographs are by the author.
Image of icon of St. Onophrius is used with permission from Aperges & Co. publishers; the hagiographer is Chris Liondas.

Book and cover design
by Michael Schrauzer

Dedicated to my wife,
Lady Natalie
of Her Majesty's Dominion of Canada

TABLE OF CONTENTS

FOREWORD xiii
PREFACE xv
INTRODUCTION xvii
PART I: THE TITULAR PATRON 1
   1. The Monastic Tradition 3
   2. Paphnutius' *Life of Onnophrus* 7
   3. Veneration of St. Onuphrius 17
PART II:
THE MONASTERY AND ITS PERSONAGES . . 21
   4. The Hermit Monks 23
   5. The Epic Poet 31
   6. The Second Apostle of Rome 47
   7. The Modern Friars 53
PART III:
A GLOBAL CHIVALRIC MOVEMENT 55
   8. History and Mission of the
      Equestrian Order 57
   9. The Order's Spiritual Center in Rome . . 65
  10. Pope Pius XII's *Motu Proprio* 71
PART IV: SELF-GUIDED TOUR 75
  11. Getting There 77
  12. Map for Self-Guided Tour 79
  13. The Exterior Grounds 81
  14. The Renaissance Loggia 85
  15. Interior Church and Chapels 95
  16. The Renaissance Cloister 123
  17. Monastery Upper Floor:
      The Museum and *Madonna* 127
CONCLUSION 131
BIBLIOGRAPHY 137
ABOUT THE AUTHOR 139
ACKNOWLEDGMENTS 141

FOREWORD

ST. ONUPHRIUS AND I, providentially, have a number of things in common. For one, his feast day falls on the date of my birth. So, when Sir John Paul Sonnen asked me to write the foreword to this excellent volume I could not resist the opportunity to write about a great saint, a magnificent church, and an order of Knights and Dames of which I am a proud member.

I feel that St. Onuphrius and I are kindred souls. He fled to the desert to find silence, prayer, and freedom from the things of this world. I, too, through entirely different circumstances, have found a desert of my own. I have found not the Thebaid, as our saint did, but the desert of my own body. In 2019, I was diagnosed with amyotrophic lateral sclerosis, or ALS for short. Since then, the lives of the Desert Fathers have become very real to me. They withdrew to caves in the desert to live in silence and stillness. There, like their Master before them, they fast and pray, as well as do battle with the demons who seek to destroy the holiness of the solitary monk. I, too, have been led by God, not to the Egyptian desert caves, but to the cave of my own body. I fast because I cannot swallow, I am still because my muscles have become so atrophied that I cannot move. I, too, like the Great Anchorites, do battle with the demons who would have me, like holy Job, "curse God, and die" (Job 2:9). St. Onuphrius has been a great companion and teacher on my own sojourn in the desert of ALS. He will also accompany you through the deserts of your own life.

Near and dear to members of the Equestrian Order of the Holy Sepulchre of Jerusalem is the church in Rome dedicated to St. Onuphrius. Nestled alongside the seven hills of Rome, it is a spiritual home in Rome for all the Knights and Dames of the Holy Sepulchre. Sadly, few are the Knights and Dames who visit there. I think that among the busy streets of Rome, and the hectic schedules of pilgrims, it would be a good respite for silence, prayer, and taking in the beauty of the Eternal City from above. Its beauty has attracted poets, saints, and those seeking wisdom through the centuries. We would do well to go where these great ones have gone before.

The Church of St. Onuphrius is the spiritual headquarters in Rome of the Equestrian Order of the Holy Sepulchre of Jerusalem. As such it is connected with the motto of the Order: *Deus lo Vult* (God Wills It). This motto has taken on a much deeper meaning for me since my diagnosis with ALS. For the crusaders of old, it meant that God willed them to give life and limb in defense of the Holy Land and its holy places. For me, now, it is a battle cry to embrace my own particular cross, for God has willed it for me. You too, dear readers, will find the will of God if you follow the way of the pilgrim set out in this volume. For it takes us on a journey to the Thebaid, to Rome, and to the Holy Land, where we encounter saints, poets, and fellow pilgrims along the way. So, forward we go, for *Deus lo Vult!*

Fr. Dana Ambrose Christensen, KHS
April 24, 2021
Feast of St. Fidelis of Sigmaringen

PREFACE

IT WAS AN ACT OF PROVIdence that led me at the age of nineteen to visit Sant'Onofrio al Gianicolo as a pilgrim while staying as a guest at the Pontifical North American College in Rome. One bright sunny morning in March 1998 as I exited the main entrance with a few friends, we decided to turn right and follow the street, which led us to Sant'Onofrio, just a few minutes' walk up the hill. It was then we discovered this rare Renaissance gem, a hidden treasure in a city of churches.

The Renaissance was a time of realization, continuity and *rebirth* that began in fifteenth-century Italy. The name *Renaissance* or *Classical* is given to that manner of building and style of ornament which is an adaptation of the models of ancient Greece and Rome. These ancient classical models helped influence the new architecture and painting of Sant'Onofrio. It is my hope this little book will inspire you, dear pilgrim, and help create a conversation among other pilgrims to venture off the beaten path to explore Sant'Onofrio, a rare legacy of the Italian Renaissance. For the pilgrim visiting Rome, as many of you do with some frequency, I recommend you make time to visit, perhaps in conjunction with a leisurely afternoon stroll on the beautiful Janiculum Hill.

The church is of special interest to Knights and Dames of the Order of the Holy Sepulchre because it is their official church in Rome, the unique spiritual home of members of the Order in the Eternal City. It is also of special interest

to anyone interested in the epic Catholic poetry of Torquato Tasso or the life of the great St. Philip Neri, who is known as the Second Apostle of Rome.

Meanwhile, the ravages of time have taken their toll on the fabric of Sant'Onofrio, and its priceless interior and exterior are once again in need of preservation and repair. Therefore, let this little book help to reawaken interest in this treasure, that it may be restored at an opportune time and brought back to its full vigor. To all visitors to Rome, I invite you to visit Sant'Onofrio as a pilgrim, in search of a message that I trust you will receive.

Buon Camino!

John Paul Sonnen, KHS
January 1, 2020
Rome Cavalieri

INTRODUCTION

THE SAYING THAT *ALL roads lead to Rome* originated from the fact that certain main roads of the Roman Empire radiated to and from Rome. Chaucer added extra meaning when he noted in his medieval instruction *A Treatise on the Astrolabe* that "diverse paths lead diverse folk the right way to Rome."[1] In Rome alone one realizes the eternal and the universal. There alone one lives at once in the whole of history. Indeed, the pilgrim's path to Rome has been paved by millions and gives an unparalleled testimony through the ages.

Sir Roger Scruton, in his seminal work *Beauty*, states that "True art appeals to the imagination"[2] and that true art "invites us to another place."[3] Indeed, Sant'Onofrio is just that — another place. In a city of over four hundred churches, it stands out as a citadel of faith overlooking Rome and as an oasis of Renaissance beauty. While the Italian Renaissance was one of the world's great ages of art, in sheer numbers of notable artists and art produced, it has bequeathed to Rome something special in the Church of Sant'Onofrio.

1. Jeffry Forgeng and Will McLean, *Daily Life in Chaucer's England*, 49.

2. Roger Scruton, *Beauty: A Very Short Introduction*, 88.

3. Ibid., 89.

SANT'ONOFRIO AL GIANICOLO (in Latin, *S. Onuphrii* or *Honuphrii in Janiculo*) was consecrated in 1513. Since then thousands of pilgrims have visited and experienced the peace of this hidden place. The author of this humble volume encourages everyone to make a visit. Readers are urged to venture off the beaten path and explore, setting out on a journey in search of a message. It is the hope of the author that this little book will provide both pleasure and sure information for the many who may wish to know something of Sant'Onofrio and its message. This church has been identified by art historians as being culturally important and is, in the opinion of the author, one of Rome's best kept secrets. Because it is perched on the northern slope of the Janiculum Hill, west of the Tiber River, and therefore outside the traditional Seven Hills district of Rome, Sant'Onofrio has been often overlooked by pilgrim and tourist itineraries. The reality is that it is news for many that Sant'Onofrio even exists.

This beautiful church has long been a favorite place with pilgrims and locals alike. Over the years, seminarians of the Pontifical North American College (located just down the street) have found Sant'Onofrio's quiet and secluded atmosphere, along with its splendid little garden and view of Rome, conducive to prayer, study and meditation. Over the years, a certain number of American and Canadian seminarians have even chosen to celebrate one of their first Masses here, as have a number of English seminarians from Rome's Venerable English College.

Sant'Onofrio is one of the few churches in Rome that is predominantly Renaissance in style. This is good news for those critics who perhaps do not care much for the Baroque, which since the Counter-Reformation has been the preponderant style of architecture seen in Rome. Baroque, as part of the Catholic response

INTRODUCTION

to the Protestant Reformation, introduced an over-the-top exuberance of forms and beauty to help inspire the faithful to greatness while giving glory to God. This style has been almost universally condemned by the historians of the period of the Enlightenment, who, while viewing the Catholic Church in general with contempt and aversion, saw the Baroque as a bit much because it lacked the simplicity of earlier Renaissance forms. The truth is, Sant'Onofrio is a slight mix that allows visitors a rare glimpse of the beauty of both. While predominantly it highlights the Renaissance principles that are epitomized by greats such as Alberti and Bramante, architects who helped bring the High Renaissance to Rome, it also — almost as an afterthought — has on display considerable Baroque influences, which are seen principally in its side chapels and funerary monuments.

THERE IS A FURTHER CONNECtion between Sant'Onofrio and the epic Renaissance poet Torquato Tasso, one of the most celebrated Catholic poets of all time. Tasso, who was from Sorrento (near Naples), visited Rome many times and spent the last month of his life as a guest at Sant'Onofrio, secluded within the walls of its hushed cloister. Readers are encouraged to get to know his most famous poem, *Jerusalem Delivered*, an epic about the drama of the First Crusade. Tasso's poetry emanated from a free creativity of the spirit that was oriented to speak and express, resulting in great words proffered. He was a perceiver, nothing having any interest to him unless he could, as it were, see and touch it with the spiritual senses, with which he was pre-eminently endowed.

The great St. Philip Neri was also fond of Sant'Onofrio church and its gardens and vineyards, where he would gather his followers in spring and summer months for relaxed spiritual enrichment, mixed with songs, mirth and cheerful recreation. Neri, who was born in Florence, was a later vocation, ordained in his mid-thirties. He moved to Rome as an adult and is known as the Second Apostle of Rome, after St. Peter, due to his pre-eminent gift for evangelizing. Neri is best remembered for his remarkable ability to walk through the city, entering into conversation with people and leading them to consider topics he set before them in the hopes of converting them. He founded a very successful society of secular clergy known as the Congregation of the Oratory, which is still going strong today in Rome and elsewhere.

Further, many pilgrims are delighted to discover the connection between Sant'Onofrio and the Order of the Holy Sepulchre, a Catholic order of knighthood founded in the wake of the First Crusade to liberate, protect and defend the tomb of Christ in Jerusalem. To this day, members of the Order pledge their help to defend the Christians in the Holy Land. Sant'Onofrio is their spiritual home in the Eternal City, officially designated by the Vatican. Members of the Order travel both to Jerusalem to see the empty tomb of Christ, the holiest shrine in Christendom, as well as to Rome, the center of Christendom, to see both Sant'Onofrio and the tomb of the Blessed Apostle Peter, located under St. Peter's Basilica.

INTRODUCTION

For centuries Christians have revered Rome as a chosen city and the bearer of a sublime destiny. The pagan heritage of the ancient capital flowered into Christian Rome in conformity with a mysterious and elevated providential plan. Upon the remains of Rome's first greatness arose the great monuments of Christian civilization. By divine dispensation, the most beautiful churches in the world were built here, a patrimony of faith that has been preserved, fostered and advanced in the universal context of pilgrimage. To Rome we travel as pilgrims, the world's most majestic city. St. John Henry Newman, who brought St. Philip Neri's legacy of the Oratory to the English-speaking world, wrote, "And now what can I say of Rome, but that it is the first of cities and that all I ever saw are but as dust compared with its majesty and glory."[4]

In Rome is found the greatest variety of pilgrims and the greatest variety of pilgrim itineraries. The mystery of the encounter of the pilgrim is best described as an encounter with beauty. This is largely through art, which is something more than just the piecing together of salient names and dates; it is primarily a consideration of Divine Revelation, eternal truths and Christian civilization. God has revealed himself through great historical patterns into which social and cultural norms have been built over the past centuries. Rather than merely a parade of time-worn images, art is part of the living tradition of the Catholic Church.

4. Wilfrid Philip Ward, *The Life of John Henry Cardinal Newman*, Volume I, 53.

Indeed, the Church in her munificence has given the world the greatest works of art on a global scale, borrowed from the genius of Greco-Roman foundations. The art she does not keep for herself but gives freely to all, maintaining it as a *communis patria*, a shared heritage belonging to all people of good will. The art of each civilization has developed within its own region, while the Roman Empire covered a vast area of land and peoples providing a seedbed of a great many artistic talents and influences. Christianity was born in the Middle East on the edge of the ancient world, and from there it grew and expanded to Rome, the heart of the Empire, where it reached an artistic and cultural flowering on European soils.

As it blossomed, Christianity possessed social, cultural and artistic characteristics that gave birth to successive ages of art. The mystical climate of Catholic Europe distinguished itself from every previous civilization pre-eminently by its art and saints. This brings to mind a quotation from Cardinal Ratzinger, "The only really effective apologia for Christianity comes down to two arguments, namely, the saints the Church has produced and the art which has grown in her womb."[5]

5. Vittorio Messori, *The Ratzinger Report*, 129.

❧While there are various spelling differentiations, here it will be St. Onuphrius, unless taken directly from a quotation or book title.

THIS BOOK IS IN FOUR PARTS. The first recounts the story of the church's titular patron, a fourth-century Egyptian monk known in Italian as Sant'Onofrio, in English generally as St. Onuphrius and in Latin as S. Onuphrio or Honuphrius—from which comes *Humphrey* (both a masculine given name

INTRODUCTION:

and a surname). The second tells of the founding of Sant'Onofrio as a monastery in Rome in the fifteenth century and of notable personages that have been associated with it. The third describes the Equestrian Order of the Holy Sepulchre of Jerusalem, whose spiritual home has been at Sant'Onofrio since 1945. The fourth is a visitor's guide to the site, describing in rich detail the history of its cultural and spiritual treasures.

PART I
The Titular Patron

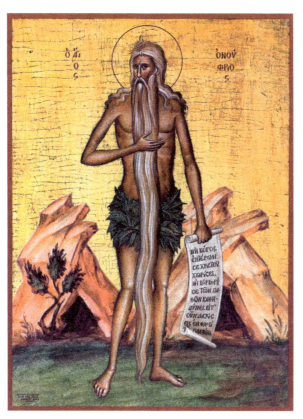

☧ Saint Onuphrius

I
The Monastic Tradition

ST. ONUPHRIUS[1] WAS a real person, an anchorite or hermit-monk, a man who lived apart from his monastery. He is easy to spot in iconography and artistic representations, always depicted as an elderly man living in the wilderness, with a very long white beard and long hair covering his body with a girdle of leaves.[2] He was one of the Desert Fathers who dwelled in seclusion in Upper Egypt in the fourth century, part of the first great expansion of Christian monasticism.[3]

THE MONASTICISM OF THE EAST spread to the West and in time produced all the fruits of a higher culture. This included a flowering of art, music and learning. "Indeed, from the seventh to the tenth century, the monasteries were the only effective educational force that survived in the Western world."[4] The monasteries passed on this information through educational activity to the general public, to those families who lived near the shelter of the monastery or to those who studied or found refuge within their protective walls. In this way, a great many souls have been touched and influenced by monasticism over the centuries.

Although most historians agree the first Christian monks were the Essenes, to whom St. John the Baptist belonged at the Dead Sea, institutional Christian monasticism was first seen

---

1. There are many sources on St. Onuphrius for those who may wish to do more study. Greek and Latin texts are available in the *Bibliotheca Hagiographica Graeca*, nn. 1378–1382, and the *B. H. Latina*, nn. 6334–6338. There is also more info in the *Acta Sanctorum*, vol. III. Oriental sources are also plentiful, notably from Coptic and Ethiopic Christians.

2. For this reason, he is considered a patron saint of weavers.

3. For a more thorough presentation of Egyptian monasticism, see Lucien Regnault, *The Day-to-Day Life of the Desert Fathers in Fourth-Century Egypt* (St. Bede's Press, 2002).

4. Christopher Dawson, *The Formation of Christendom*, 187.

in the deserts of Egypt in the fourth century. There, the first generations of monks, including St. Onuphrius, lived a kind of spiritual martyrdom in the seclusion of the lonely desert frontier. Their lives and example showed people the way one comes to God. The locals called them citizens of the desert. Monks went to live in the desert on account of God and to be closer to God. In monastic literature, both *desert* and *mountain* have a geographical and religious sense. The monastic desert is embraced by the Coptic word *toou*, which signifies both mountain and desert; in Greek, respectively, *eremos*, a solitary place, and *ors*, a mountain. Physically, the desert and mountains for Egyptian monks poised them between civilization and wasteland. The desolate arid land of the desert was at the base of the mountains, between the arable Nile and the howling wilderness beyond. "The Egyptian desert ends abruptly in the escarpment overlooking the flat valley floor of the Nile. Oros is therefore barren, uncultivated land, not necessarily rising to any height, as against the irrigated zone of the valley and delta."[5]

The desert was understood geographically, spiritually and mystically as a harsh and uncompromising place where Christian hermits could be a microcosm of Christian culture, perfected by God through hardship and temptation with total trust in God. Spiritually and psychologically, the monastic desert was a paradox. Going out to the barren desert was entering the fertile land of the spiritual life. The stark landscape and barren shadows of the desert revealed an immediate threat and challenge, with temptations from the evil one — and the saving power of God. The

5. Norman Russell, *The Lives of the Desert Fathers*, 125.

locals told stories and legends of monks of the desert who were ministered to by the angels. Withdrawing from cities and towns, the monks who set out to leave civilization produced *cities* of monks that attracted both monks and visitors and sent hermits out into the remote deserts. The desert was far from Alexandria, the early cradle of Egyptian Christianity. It was far removed from the established monasteries of the Roman Province of Thebais, which had been founded by Diocletian in Upper Egypt and was under Roman law. It was infinitely remote from Rome, the heart of the Roman Empire. There on the edge of the Empire lay garrison towns such as Aswan and Philae, where Christians coexisted and lived amid pagan remnants of the pre-Christian world.

In the fourth century, it was still a common sight to see pagans maintaining temples and shrines amid the multiplying Christian churches. The monks in the desert were integral to the Christian community as intercessors, contemplatives, mystics and wonder-workers. Those monks who chose not to enter the desert understood that the desert does not have to be a geographical reality. Meanwhile, they referenced the Scriptures, which illustrated many stories of the desert. The people of Israel wandered in the desert. Saints such as Elijah, Elisha and John the Baptist lived and prophesied in the desert, while even Christ made His way into the desert. The monk would enter the desert to encounter God and triumph over the temptations of the world, flesh and devil.

Thus, the monks laid the foundations of Christian culture in the East. In fact, no other factor so profoundly influenced the development

PART I: THE TITULAR PATRON

❧ Also in the West, it should be duly noted, the famous Abbey of Our Lady of Fontgombault in the Creuse River Valley of France comes to mind, where the first monks had been hermits living in caves along the side of the river, still visible today. The group had a *Magister Eremitarum* (Hermit-Master), who founded it, a monk named Gombaud, who was succeeded by another until the monastery was formally set up in the Benedictine tradition in the year 1091.

of Christian culture in the East. The early monks and monasteries were nothing but a simple and modest pattern of Christian culture. They had a defined social form, a high spiritual end and independent economic foundation. They based their lives on the radical refusal to compromise with fallen human nature. Their monastic lives were based on strictly disciplining the three main instincts that permeated the secularist society of the Roman Empire: the sexual impulse, the economic impulse and the power impulse. These three dominating themes of the prevalent culture were excluded by the threefold (Christian) monastic vows of poverty, chastity and obedience. Thus, the monastic culture, from which came great saints who persevered, is still in existence as an institution and carries on its influence even today.

The monastic apostolate was especially suited as a counter to the conditions of the barbarian society of the ancient world. It provided little oases of Christian light amid the destruction and anarchy of the pagan world. The monks lived in little self-contained worlds, each a school of the service of the Lord in which it was possible to live freely a Christian life without having to surrender to the lower standards of the secular culture. The existence of the monks presupposed a social code that said, in effect, candidates were to give their entire lives as an oblation. Each hermit's cave or monk's monastery formed a hidden pocket of peace, a cell of Christian culture that survived in a barbarous world and leads us to the man, St. Onuphrius.

2
Paphnutius' Life of Onnophrius

EVERYTHING WE know about the life of St. Onuphrius comes from the Abbot St. Paphnutius, a fellow monk who led an ascetical life in the Thebaid desert in Egypt. The account he has left of St. Onuphrius, *The Life of Onnophrus*, includes the life of other fourth-century hermits whom the author encountered—including Abba Timothy, whom he met just before Onuphrius. Through his story of his meeting with the saint,[1] readers catch a glimpse of the nature of the hidden holiness and trust of Onuphrius, seen only by God. This example of monastic literature brings to mind in some ways the lives of the monastic founders that were later recorded, such as the life of St. Anthony by St. Athanasius, or those of St. Benedict, St. Columban, St. Columba, Bede's *Lives of the Abbots*, or any number of other examples.

The Abbot tells of the life and ascetic feats of Onuphrius, and how the Lord above cared for him and gave him the grace to persevere, amid a long life of difficult monastic living in the wilderness, and amid great isolation from all other humans. The Abbot relates that an angel carried the Blessed Sacrament to Onuphrius every Saturday and Sunday while he lived in the desert.

---

1. It should be noted there are slightly different versions of the same story that have been redacted over the centuries, while the details remain essentially the same.

PART I: THE TITULAR PATRON

THE STORY OF ONUPHRIUS BEGINS with the Abbot, who is led into the farthest reaches of the Egyptian desert in search of any brother monks—other holy ascetics who would give profit to his soul. After days going into the most remote parts of the desert and encountering another hermit-monk, Timothy, the Abbot was finally led to Onuphrius.

After walking for days in a state of exhaustion, suddenly he looked and saw a man in the distance. The man's hair was so long it spread out over his body. His loins were covered by leaves of desert plants. This man was Onuphrius, the great desert-dweller and fellow monk. The Abbot was afraid and climbed up on a ledge of the mountain. The elder Onuphrius approached him, near death from hunger and thirst and said, "Come down to me, holy man. I too am a man of the desert, like yourself. I live in this desert on account of my sins. You too are a friend of God."[2]

The Abbot came down and sat with the saint, asking his name. Onuphrius responded, while explaining that he had originally come from a monastery of monks: "My name is Onnophrius, and for sixty years I have lived in this desert. I walk in the mountains like a wild beast and I never see anyone I recognize. Now I lived in a monastic community on the mountain of Shmoun in the Thebaid.[3] The name of the monastery was Etete. We were all of one mind and lived in accord with one another, and peace dwelled in our midst. We lived together a life of quiet contemplation,

2. Tim Vivian, *Paphnutius: Histories of the Monks of Upper Egypt and The Life of St. Onnophrius*, 151.

3. Hermopolis Magna of the Greeks.

CHAPTER 2: PAPHNUTIUS' LIFE OF ONNOPHRIUS

glorifying God. Now I would spend the night in vigil with them, and I learned from them the rules of God. The great ones were perfect as the angels of the Lord are perfect."[4]

Because Onuphrius had lived before in a monastery, monastic life was second nature to him. He had received the proper training and instruction in his younger years from brother monks who acted as mentors. They had told him stories of other hermits in the desert who were well known in Bible stories, receiving help from God through divine assistance. Onuphrius longed to share in this life and received his inspiration from them. The other monks told him stories of the biblical characters Elijah and John the Baptist, "I heard them speaking about our father Elijah the Tishbite, saying that in every way he was powerful in God. There lived in this desert also John the Baptist: of those born of woman, none has arisen greater than he. He lived in desert places until the day of his manifestation to Israel."[5]

The young Onuphrius said to the other monks, "My fathers, aren't then those who live in the desert the elect — more so than we? Look, we see each other every day and we gather together for worship. When we're hungry we have the benefit of food prepared for us; when we're thirsty we have the benefit of water to drink. When we're weak the brothers help us and when we want a plate or a pot to eat from we serve each other out of love for God. Where will those who live in the desert on account of God find anyone if they run into trouble? Or if they are hungry where will they find food; if they are thirsty where will they find water to drink"?[6]

[4] *Ibid.*, 152.

[5] *Ibid.*, 152.

[6] *Ibid.*, 152.

The response from the brother monks was that those living as hermits have a difficult life, with many hardships including temptations from the devil. However, the monks responded to him that anchorites greatly rejoiced on account of hunger and thirst and their manner of life. Therefore, the adversary, the devil who fights against them to tempt them, did not want them to continue their lifestyle as hermits because he knew that great was the reward which they would receive when they died and left the body for Heaven. Only when the anchorites endured did the mercies of God establish themselves in them. The monks shared with the young Onuphrius, now aspiring to be a hermit, the news that God himself caused the angels to serve the hermits with food and he brought them water from the rock.

Hearing these stories, the young man was deeply inspired knowing that hermits are pursuing the life of perfection, comforted at all times and in all needs by Heavenly angels. Convinced this call was for him, he set out from the monastery for the desert, guided by a light, his guardian angel, who was to assure him all would be well. He writes of his inspiration and conviction, "And I, your brother, when I had heard these things from these perfect ones of God, they became like honey sweet to my soul and I was filled within with complete understanding: I became like those whose minds travel to another world. I immediately got up; I took a few loaves of bread with me, sufficient for a journey of four days, so I would have something to eat until I reached the place which the Lord would determine for me. Now when I had left my monastery, I looked and I saw a light before me.

I was afraid, and thought to myself that I would turn back to where I first had come and remain the way I was. When he saw that I was afraid, he said to me, 'Do not be afraid. I am the angel who has dwelled with you and walked with you since you were a child. You will carry through to its completion this stewardship which the Lord has appointed for you.'"[7]

Onuphrius, longing to share in the life in the desert where hermits lived in solitude in caves and huts, entered the mountains and walked in the desert for six or seven miles until he saw his first inhabited cave. Seeing there was a person inside, he waited. Out emerged a hermit, a great saint of God, whose face shone with grace and beauty. Onuphrius knelt at his feet but was raised up and greeted by the monk who called him by name, saying to him, "You are Onnophrius, my fellow-worker in the Lord. Come in; the Lord be with you. You will succeed in the good work to which he has called you."[8] With this, Onuphrius went in and stayed with the monk for a few days, learning from him about God and how to do the spiritual works of the desert.

As soon as the seasoned hermit saw that Onuphrius understood the hidden and fearful fighting that takes place in the desert, he took him to a desolate place further in the desert where the young man was to live by himself for the sake of God. The old man said to the young man: "Since the Lord God has appointed you to this work, you must live in the desert."[9] With this the old man immediately arose and walked with him into the desert on a journey of four days. Finally they came to a small hut. There the elder monk instructed Onuphrius that this was the place which the Lord had appointed for him to

7. Ibid., 154.

8. Ibid., 154.

9. Ibid., 155.

live. The man stayed with him for a month until the young man was ready and capable to do the good work — struggling for the Lord — which it was time for him to do. Afterwards the elder left and the two did not see each other for a year until the old man laid down his body and Onuphrius buried him at his home.

Onuphrius had a great many struggles in the desert, including hunger, thirst and weather. He recounted to the Abbot these difficulties and the food he ate, including help he received from the angels. "I suffered a great deal on numerous occasions from hunger and thirst and from the fiery heat outside during the day and the great frost at night. My flesh wasted away because of the dew of Heaven. Now when God saw that I patiently endured in the good fight of fasting and that I devoted myself completely to ascetic practices, he had his holy angels serve me with my daily food; he gave it to me at night and strengthened my body. And the palm tree produced for me twelve bunches of dates each year, and I would eat one bunch each month. And he also made the plants that grow in the desert sweet as honey in my mouth. For it is written, 'A person shall not live by bread alone, but by every word which proceeds from the mouth of God shall a person live' [Matthew 4:4; Luke 4:4]. If you do the will of God, he will care for you wherever you are, for he has said in the Holy Gospel: 'Take no care for what you will eat or what you will drink or what you will clothe yourself with. Your father in Heaven knows what you need without your asking him. Instead, seek his kingdom and his righteousness and these things will be added unto you' [Matthew 6:31–33]."[10]

10. Ibid., 156.

CHAPTER 2: PAPHNUTIUS' LIFE OF ONNOPHRIUS

Speaking of the Holy Eucharist brought to him by angels, Onuphrius explained some of the mystical experiences of the monks, including that the angels brought the Blessed Eucharist to the desert hermits who lived alone in seclusion, "My holy father, an angel of God comes and gives me the Eucharist on the Sabbath and the Lord's Day; and to everyone in the desert who lives there on account of God and sees no human being, the angel comes and gives the Eucharist and comforts them. What's more, if they desire to see anyone, they are taken up into the Heavenly places where they see all the saints and greet them, and their hearts are filled with light; they rejoice and are glad with God in those good things. Now when they are seen they are comforted and they completely forget that they have suffered. Afterwards, they return to their bodies and they continue to feel comforted for a long time. If they travel to another world through the joy which they have seen, they do not even remember this world exists."[11]

11. *Ibid.*, 156.

Hearing this news, the Abbot was overjoyed and greatly rejoiced that he was able to hear these things from Onuphrius while seeing his holy face and hearing his sweet words. This caused him to forget momentarily the sufferings he had undergone on his journey through the mountain. Strength returned to his body and and soul. Next the two men walked together two or three miles to his hut where Onuphrius lived in the wilderness. The Abbot remarked it was a wonder to behold the blessed old man as an athlete. When they entered in the hut they prayed together. When they finished they talked some more. When the sun was about to set, they ate dinner together, bread and water. Next, they spent the night in prayer until morning.

When morning came, the Abbot noticed the face of Onuphrius had been changed, transformed as though he had become a different person. His countenance had turned into fire and this greatly frightened the Abbot. Onuphrius said to the Abbot, "Do not be afraid, my brother in God, for the Lord has sent you to care for my body and bury it. Indeed, this very day I shall complete my stewardship and go to the place of everlasting rest [...] when you go to Egypt, proclaim my memory as fragrant incense to the brethren. Whoever makes an offering in my name and in memory of me, Jesus himself will bring him [into the feast] in the first hour of a thousand years."[12]

The question arose if the Abbot should stay and remain as a hermit, taking the place of Onuphrius. The Abbot then asked if he could be at his side when Onuphrius departed from his body. The saint responded, "No, my son, for you have not been appointed to this stewardship, but the Lord has appointed you to comfort the holy brothers who live in the desert, to proclaim their sweet fragrance among the brethren who worship God as a benefit to those who listen to you. Now go to Egypt, my son, and persevere in the good work."[13]

The Abbot responded, "Bless me, my father, that I may stand before God and as I have been worthy to see you on earth so may I be worthy to see you in the other world before the Lord Jesus Christ."[14]

Onuphrius responded, "My son, may God not cause you to grieve about anything and may he strengthen you in his love, so that you neither turn away nor fall but succeed in the

12. *Ibid.*, 158.

13. *Ibid.*, 159.

14. *Ibid.*, 159.

CHAPTER 2: PAPHNUTIUS' LIFE OF ONNOPHRIUS

work which you have undertaken. May the angels shelter you and deliver you ... and may no accusation fall on you when you come to meet God."[15]

When he had finished saying these blessed things, Onuphrius stood up and prayed to God with sighs and many tears. Then he lay down on the ground and completed his earthly journey, his stewardship of God, giving up his spirit into the hands of God on the sixteenth of Paone (June 10). The Abbot recounts the scene with the sound of angels: "And I heard the voices of angels singing hymns before the blessed Abba Onnophrius and there was great gladness when he came to meet God."[16]

Finally, the Abbot took off his cloak and tore it in two. One piece he kept for himself and the other he used as a burial shroud. He wrapped the corpse of the saint and laid him in a cleft in the rock. At that point he heard the voices from Heaven of a multitude of angels rejoicing and crying out, "Alleluia"! The Abbot pronounced his prayer over the body and rolled several stones over him. When he next stood up and prayed again, the palm tree that fed the saintly hermit fell down to the ground. He took this as a sign that it was not God's will that he remain. Greatly amazed at the series of events, the Abbot consumed what was left of the bread and water and left on his way to return to civilization.

Thus concludes the simple and yet inspiring story of the life and ascetic practice of the holy hermit St. Onuphrius the Anchorite, by the Abbot Paphnutius.

15. *Ibid.*, 159.

16. *Ibid.*, 159.

3
Veneration of St. Onuphrius

HE *ROMAN MARTYR-ology*, which aims to help Catholics cherish the lives of the saints and develop a genuine *pietas* (pious devotion) toward the men and women who laid the foundations for Christianity in the East and West, has this entry for June 12, the feast day of St. Onuphrius in the Latin Church: "In Egypt, St. Onuphrius, an anchorite, who for sixty years lived a religious life in a vast desert, and, famous for great virtues and merits, passed into Heaven. His mighty deeds were recorded by the Abbot Paphnutius."[1]

The cult of devotion to St. Onuphrius is an ancient one from the East, which became popular in the West in the Middle Ages. It is still existent and strong in some places, including Egypt, Greece and Byzantium, Portugal, Sicily and other parts of southern Italy. Purported relics of the saint exist, and one is kept in the church of Sant'Onofrio in Rome. Others are said to be kept in Constantinople, Lavriv (Ukraine) and Brunswick (Germany).

St. Onuphrius is remembered today as a great spiritual guide whose story, similar to that of other desert monks, helped shape and inspire the Christian Church while it was emerging as the dominant faith of the Roman Empire.

This saint is venerated in both the Orthodox and Catholic Churches and merits great attention and renown. There are stories and legends told about him by Coptic Christians in Egypt

1. Canon J. B. O'Connell, Editor, *The Roman Martyrology*, 121.

that have been passed on from generation to generation. Egyptian Copts speak of miracles and signs and wonders wrought by his holy intercession. A discourse homily on him by Pisentius of Coptos (568–632) is customarily read on his feast day in Coptic communities. This document is one of the best of its kind in the area of Coptic letters. Although it tells us nothing new about the saint, the sermon shows that already in about A. D. 600 the feast of St. Onuphrius was celebrated with great solemnity.

Images of the saint are rare. One of the more famous paintings depicting St. Onuphrius is entitled *The Madonna with Child Between Saints Flavian and Onuphrius,* an oil painting by Lorenzo Lotto, completed in the year 1508. Today, it is on display in the Borghese Gallery in Rome. The painting has an interesting bit of history. On the right of the painted image of Our Lady is St. Onuphrius the hermit, with St. Flavian on the other side. The character of St. Onuphrius is said to have been possibly inspired by an elderly-looking character from the Temple in Jerusalem depicted in Dürer's *Christ among the Doctors,* which the German artist had painted in Venice in 1506.

The memory of how St. Onuphrius lived in secluded prayer as a hermit-monk inspires hermits to do the same in the East today. Small Coptic monasteries abound in Egypt. Various monasteries throughout the Christian world have been named after him. In Lviv, Ukraine, there exists a Basilian monastery named after the saint with a beautiful and inspired history and monastery complex. There is also a second St. Onuphrius Monastery in Ukraine, located in the small Carpathian village of Lavriv, from which devotion to the saint spread among local peasant populations. This fervor has endured today among not a few of the farming families in Eastern Europe. In eastern Poland near the Belarusian border there is also an Orthodox monastery in the village of Jabłeczna, dedicated to St. Onuphrius. This medieval foundation came about in the year 1498 when, according to folklore, an icon of the saint was found floating down the local river, seen by villagers as a manifestation of God's special grace.

❧ Carven stone image of Sant'Onofrio from above the entrance of monastery in Jerusalem

In Jerusalem a very well-known Orthodox monastery for nuns is also named in honor of the saint. This monastic complex was built in 1892 in an area known in biblical times as the Potter's Field. This is the piece of land that Judas Iscariot is said to have purchased with the thirty pieces of silver obtained by his betrayal of Jesus, recorded in Acts 1:18–19. Tourist buses drive by on the southern slope of the Gehenna Valley to point out this interesting historical place, just outside the Old City of Jerusalem.

PART I: THE TITULAR PATRON

The main entrance of the monastery has above its doorway a carving in stone of St. Onuphrius, bowing to an angel; the saint is easily recognizable by his long beard and leaves around his loins and legs.

PART II
The Monastery and its Personages

❧ Torquato Tasso
(engraved portrait)

❧ Wooden statue of St. Philip Neri at the Church of St. Mark in Saint Paul, Minnesota

4
The Hermit Monks

ALTHOUGH THE institution of Christian monasticism was of purely Oriental origin and came into existence in the Egyptian desert in the fourth century, it was in the West and especially in Italy that this development produced the most remarkable fruits. Catholic historian Christopher Dawson speaks of the spread of monasticism which had its sources in the East: "The Church accepted this new way of life as an essential expression of the Christian spirit and spread it East and West from the Atlantic to the Black Sea and the Persian Gulf. And as it grew it adapted itself to the life of the different peoples amongst whom it came, though it remained fully conscious of its origins and of the continuity of its tradition."[1]

Sant'Onofrio in Rome is symbolic of the link between monasticism in the East (Egypt) and the West (Rome). It was established in 1419 when the Order of Poor Hermits of St. Jerome was founded by Blessed Nicolo di Forca Palena (1349–1449) and Blessed Pietro Gambacorta (1355–1435). The proximity to the Vatican ensured that the community received attention and patronage. The monks were also known as the Hieronymites, which in the past has led to some confusion with the Spanish monastic order of the same name.

Both men had already been hermit monks and professed members of the Third Order of St. Francis when they founded their new order of

1. Christopher Dawson, *Christianity and European Culture*, 102.

PART II: THE MONASTERY AND ITS PERSONAGES

hermits on Rome's Janiculum Hill. Both had also been previously noted for their penitential acts and austere methods of life. When they decided with several companions to create a hermitage in pursuit of a life of solitude in Rome, they settled upon the northern edge of the Janiculum Hill because in those years it was secluded.

In those days, the land where the monastery was located was a quiet, wooded holm oak grove high up on a steep and inaccessible hill. A donkey track existed along the ridge of the hill west of the complex that led visitors to the site for many years. In addition, there was a very steep footpath, the present Via di Sant'Onofrio, that plunged down the hill on the eastern side to the Tiber River. In 1446 a rough and steep driveway was built to their monastery, presently known as the Salita di Sant'Onofrio.

While the order received initial approval from Pope Martin V in 1420, full approval came from Pope Eugene IV in 1446, "It was Eugene IV who presented to the Order of Hieronymites the newly founded church and monastery of S. Onofrio on the Janiculum, where the stricken poet Tasso was later given shelter."[2] Fame of the community spread, especially because hermetical and monastic life in Rome during that period had been in decline. The monks' first hut in the wood housing was replaced with a proper monastery and church, begun in 1439 and completed in 1444. With the new monastic complex the community grew in size and stature.

In those days, the monastic community was the great social institution by which the Church carried out its work of Christian acculturation, dominating the whole development of medieval culture and beyond. Each monastery was a

2. Roloff Beny and Peter Gunn, *The Churches of Rome*, 129.

24

CHAPTER 4: THE HERMIT MONKS

specialized organ of the Church, dedicated to the performance of some particular spiritual task. The monks of Sant'Onofrio were devoted to the task of their patron, St. Onuphrius of Egypt, living as simple hermits hidden in prayer. This was their mandate, the timeless ideal and universal spirit of the apostolate for which they were founded. From the beginning, the monks were faithful to their hermetical call: "Their principal work was study and exegesis of the Scriptures, and the life was eminently one of retirement."[3] Meanwhile, in later years the order exploded in growth in Spain: "The great Spanish province, which formerly had the Guadalupe, Belen, Escurial and 55 other monasteries, was proscribed and dissolved in 1836 [the result of Masonic revolution]. The remnant of the order came to an end in 1933."[4]

In 1435 Blessed Pietro Gambacorta died before the completion of the new church and monastery. He is buried at the Church of St. Jerome in Venice. In 1449, at the venerable age of one hundred, Blessed Nicola da Forca Palena passed away in the newly built monastery. He is entombed inside the high altar of Sant'Onofrio, which he helped to establish. The Poor Hermits of St. Jerome grew in number at Sant'Onofrio from the fifteenth to the sixteenth centuries. Meanwhile, in 1568 Pope St. Pius V granted to the hermits new constitutions that required the members to take solemn vows and adhere to the Rule of St. Augustine.

After the church and monastic complex were completed in 1444, a program of interior decoration of the church began. The oldest works inside the church date from this period, 1513. In 1517, Pope Leo X granted the church

3. Donald Attwater, *A Catholic Dictionary*, 228.

4. *Ibid.*, 228.

PART II: THE MONASTERY AND ITS PERSONAGES

❧ The most important churches in Rome are titular churches. *Tituli* is an honorary designation, a time-honored custom with roots in a division made by the popes among the districts in Rome in the earliest years of Christianity. Thus was instituted over time the division of cardinals, many who were honorarily given Roman churches with titles, a tradition still celebrated at Sant'Onofrio (see Self-Guided Tour, 8).

❧ "View from Sant'Onofrio in Rome," by Rudolf von Alt, the Leopold Museum, Vienna

titular status with a cardinal deacon assigned to it. In 1588 the title was made presbyteral, with cardinal-priests assigned, a great benefice to the community. In that same year, 1588, the interior decoration was finally completed.

☩

ALTHOUGH SANT'ONOFRIO was originally the oratory of a hermitage, today the days of hermitages in the West are all but gone, in large part the general result of monks living in community where they can be answerable to each other, ruled by approved constitutions.

In 1870, as a direct result of the unfortunate episode of the Masonic-fueled revolution in Italy, the new Italian government confiscated Church properties everywhere, including the monastery of Sant'Onofrio. In 1873 the new government converted the monastery into a children's hospital, although the buildings were totally unsuitable for this purpose. In 1929, Sant'Onofrio church and monastery were received back from the government, thanks to the Lateran Concordat, a treaty signed between the Italian State and the Holy See.

Today the Ospedale Pediatrico Bambino Gesù, founded in 1869 and given to the Vatican in 1924, occupies much of the land where the monastery was once located (west of the current property). That part of the monastic complex, tragically, has since been demolished to accommodate hospital additions. Unfortunately, parts of the historic monastery that were demolished for additions included two beautiful Renaissance cloisters of the monastery, both on the west side of the church. One was north of the main cloister of today and the other to the west. Today the hospital area with its modern buildings is part of the Vatican City State, extraterritorial land that is administered by the Holy See. In the years since the revolution of Italy in 1870, the monks of Sant'Onofrio had all but died out. After the revolution only a handful were allowed by the Italian state to retain possession of the church. Without a proper monastery, vocations plummeted. The Poor Hermits of St. Jerome, after being in a state of terminal decline for many years, were finally dissolved under Pope Pius XI on January 12, 1933. The hermits of Sant'Onofrio are remembered for their penitential acts and austere methods that defined their ascetic life while also preserving devotion to St. Onuphrius.

THE LIFE OF HERMIT MONKS continues in the West, after a fashion. St. Benedict (c. 480–547) addresses anchorite monks in *The Rule*, where he grafted the best monastic inheritance and knowledge from both the East and West. In it he describes four kinds of monks. The first and most common are cenobites, monks who live in monasteries under a rule and an abbot. Then he goes on to describe hermits, those who go and live alone in solitude. He writes, "The second are the anchorites: hermits, that is, who, not in the first fervor of their religious life but after long probation in the monastery, have learned by the help and experience of others to fight against the devil; and going forth well-armed from the ranks of their brethren to the single-handed combat of the desert, are now able to fight safely without the support of others, by their own strength under God's aid, against the vices of the flesh and their evil thoughts."[5]

In those early years of monasticism, hermits were much more common in both East and West and it was easy enough to become one. All a discerning man had to do was find a suitable master to give him a habit and his blessing, a suitable site for a hermitage and some means of supplying himself with food and provisions. The Church certainly did not frown on this lifestyle. In those early years, there was not yet the promulgation of a universal Code of Canon Law for the Latin or Eastern Churches, to regulate conditions. In fact, the first experience of St. Benedict himself in the monk's life was as a hermit. The young Benedict had received from the monk Romanus his *melota*, the habit of sheepskin that had been adopted originally by the Egyptian monks as their distinctive dress. When St. Benedict writes of the trials of eremitical life, he speaks with first-hand knowledge as he lived this lifestyle as a young

5. Hubert van Zeller, O. S. B., *The Holy Rule*, 24.

monk, praying and working for three years in solitude at Subiaco, near Rome.

At the same time, Benedict views monks who live in a community as the strongest sort of monks (*fortissimum genus*) because there is structure, authority and accountability. He does not look upon his own early experiment as one to be imitated by others. As a general rule, for a man to step straight from the world into the desert, he believes, would be folly. St. Gregory says that time, not fervor, is the true test of desires. Candidates must first get over their early enthusiasm. St. Benedict insists first on a course of preliminary training which will both expose the traps which particularly endanger such a life and at the same time test the authenticity of so unusual a call. St. Benedict was concerned that solitude could exercise an attraction that could wholly mislead a soul. Escaping worldly care, from authority, from the drudgery of household routine, etc. "Countless illustrations could be drawn from the lives of the fathers of the desert to show how deceptive the call to isolation can be. Eccentricity, delusion, heresy even, will spring up in the desert; in a community these dangers will normally be avoided. St. Benedict is not against the eremitical life as such — in fact he provides for it — but he wants to make sure that it is embarked upon in the right dispositions."[6] Therefore hermits still exist, even in the Latin Church, although regularized and under certain conditions with the permission and blessing of an abbot.

In the history of the Catholic Church, the monastery and friary have always been set apart as a microcosm of Christian culture, an island which preserves and carries on the traditions

6. *Ibid.*, 25.

of high culture and classical learning on which the continuity of Western culture depends. The Catholic Church comes not only as the teacher of a new faith, but also as the bearer of a higher culture. The traditions of Christian education and learning, morality, books and writing, polite manners, literature, music and liturgy, art and architecture and poetry will always live in monasteries, including the friary of Sant'Onofrio. Through the darkest of days these monastic institutions will always survive, as in past centuries, due to their withdrawal from secular business and their radical life of continuous prayer, work and study in the peace and tranquility of monastic seclusion.

5
The Epic Poet

THE CHURCH OF SANT' Onofrio is perhaps best remembered as the location of the final home and resting place of the most illustrious poet of the Italian Renaissance, Torquato Tasso (1544–1595). Tasso ironically died in the monastery on the eve before he was due to be crowned with laurels as *king of poets* by Pope Clement VIII on Rome's Capitoline Hill. Similarly, in the early Renaissance the poet Petrarch had been crowned Rome's poet laureate in 1341. Although Tasso did not live to be crowned such, he was buried in a Roman toga with a crown of laurels, and angels are depicted on his tomb bringing to him laurel crowns in death.

For his epic romantic Renaissance poetry Tasso is renowned in life as in death. The Catholic Church has long been the mother of poets no less than of saints, and the best of poetry has grown in her soil thanks to creative minds like Tasso. Indeed, Tasso's influence on poetry is still felt today. The influences that helped to form his works were classical, inspired by and adapting the literary form especially of the epics of Homer and Virgil. His best remembered poem is an epic account of the First Crusade, *Gerusaleme Liberata* (Jerusalem Delivered — also known as the Liberation of Jerusalem). This poem was completed in his thirty-first year, first published in 1581. Its 1,917 stanzas are written in *ottava rima*, a rhyming stanza, with stanzas grouped in twenty cantos of varying length. For the prototype of

PART II: THE MONASTERY AND ITS PERSONAGES

the story Tasso chose Virgil and for his subject he chose the thrilling First Crusade.

The poem occupies a large space in the history of European literature and has passed immediately into the rank of classics. The commanding qualities of the work reveal Tasso's genius and individuality, beloved by generations and persons of culture and all those akin to lyrical graces. Tasso aimed quite successfully at ennobling the Italian epic style by preserving a great story with a strict unity of plot and heightened poetic diction. The story is long. The audio book of the poem in English lasts about twelve hours.

The story depicts a creative version of the combat of the siege of Jerusalem during the First Crusade, when the Christian armies were making their pilgrimage to the holy city. The work is clearly influenced by patriotic motives, showing the knights defending the Christian populace and restoring freedom to the Holy Sepulchre.

That being said, the poem is a dramatized fictional work of immense extravagance of the imagination. The work is not at all intended to be a historical account. Readers notice the similarities with the *Aeneid* by Virgil, especially with the main character and hero of the First Crusade, Godfrey of Bouillon (Goffredo), in the person of Virgil's pious Aeneas. In exquisite verse the poem sings of the deeds of the brave Crusaders and knights who struggled to restore peace and freedom to pilgrims who had sought free passage to the Holy Sepulchre in Jerusalem. There is found the tomb of Christ, impossible to destroy because it is a cave, the holiest shrine in the world, where Christ rose from the dead after three days in the ground.

CHAPTER 5: THE EPIC POET

The poem resonated through the centuries, speaking of lost love and epic heroes, greatness of characters torn between duty and their hearts, with romance, valor and honor as the central sources of lyrical passion.

While the story is infused with the fervor of religion and a knightly concept of the nominal hero, Godfrey of Bouillon, Tasso adorned the poem with a number of romantic episodes, which have certainly proved more popular and memorable than the grand sweep of the main crusader theme. Thus, while the climax of the epic is the capture of the holy city of Jerusalem, the reader is attracted to other characters such as Ruggiero, Rinaldo and Tancredi, as well as the Moslems with whom the Christians clash in love and war.

The stories of the poem rivet the attention of all who read of the adventures, battles, religious ceremonies, twists and turns, conclaves and stratagems. And not only of the male characters, but also, most importantly, of the female characters. Tasso's great contribution as an artist was specifically the poetry of sentiment. Sentiment, distinguished from sentimentality, is what pushed the poem to the top, giving value to what is immortal. This was something new at that time in the sixteenth century, something concordant with growing feelings for feminine characters and the ascendant art of music. In fact, the female characters became household names across Europe in the seventeenth and eighteenth centuries. The sentiment for woman — refined, natural, noble, steeped in feminine genius, melancholy, graceful, pathetically touching — breathes throughout the episodes of the poem. The cadence of the verse draws the reader toward these strong and appealing heroines.

The action of the epic turns on three stories of interaction between the Crusaders and noble pagan women of great beauty. A beautiful witch named Armida is sent by the infernal senate to sow discord in the Christian camp. Instead, she is converted to the Catholic faith by her admiration for a knight and quits the scene with a phrase of Our Lady on her tongue. Clorinda, a brave female warrior, dons armor, fights a duel with her devoted lover, and receives baptism at his hands as she is dying. Finally, there is Erminia, who is hopelessly in love with Tancredi, who steals Clorinda's armor, hoping to be able to disguise and enter the Christian camp and win the heart of her beloved.

Tasso is the link between antiquity and modernity. He unites the intellectual and aesthetic culture of Hellenism with the spiritual ideals of Christianity. The true origins of Christian poetry predate Tasso and reach as far back as the Latin tradition. There it becomes evident how in the early Church the tradition of Hebrew psalmody met the tradition of classical Latin poetry, and how their meeting produced poetic hymns and the like, which are part of a living literary form even until today. His spiritual insights are uniquely fostered by his Catholic identity. In the words of Cardinal Newman, "The Church herself is the most sacred and august of poets."[1]

While Tasso is one among a host of lyrical poets, such as Spenser, Milton and the Dutchman

[1] *Essays Critical and Historical*, 2.

CHAPTER 5: THE EPIC POET

Vondel, his works are a prime example of some the best Western religious poetry before the Baroque age, at which point much poetry began to change, critics have asserted, disfigured by excess ornament. A striking expression can be found in the following passage from Leonardo Bruni (1369–1444), a Renaissance humanist who is considered the first modern historian:

"We know, however, that in certain quarters — where all knowledge and appreciation of Letters is wanting — this whole branch of Literature, marked as it is by something of the Divine, and fit, therefore, for the highest place, is decreed as unworthy of study. But when we remember the value of the best poetry, its charm of form and the variety and interest of its subject-matter, when we consider the ease with which from our childhood up it can be committed to memory, when we recall the peculiar affinity of rhythm and meter to our emotions and our intelligence, we must conclude that Nature herself is against such headlong critics. Have we not often felt the sudden uplifting of the Soul when in the solemn Office of the Church such a passage as the *Primo dierum omnium* bursts upon us? It is not hard for us, then, to understand what the Ancients meant when they said that the Soul is ordered in special relation to the principles of Harmony and Rhythm, and is, therefore, by no other influence so fitly and so surely moved. Hence I hold my conviction to be securely based; namely that Poetry has, by our very constitution, a stronger attraction for us than any other form of expression, and that anyone ignorant of, and indifferent to, so valuable an aid to knowledge and so ennobling a source of pleasure can by no means be entitled to be called educated."[2]

[2] Leonardo Bruni D'Arezzo, *De Studiis et Leteris*, translated by W. H. Woodward, 123.

Some historians tend to minimize the importance of Renaissance poetry and its effects upon European literary culture. The truth is that the Renaissance was original and influential, and this is also reflected in its poetry. The Renaissance marked both the birth of the modern world and the self-discovery of modern man. It marked an epoch-marking change in Western culture that is reflected in the literature of the time. The Renaissance was not merely a revival of classical studies or classical traditional culture of the Hellenistic and Roman world. It was the coming of a new culture, combining the two, with roots deep in the past and which had been developing for centuries before it achieved its full expression in fifteenth-century Italy. Tasso's *Jerusalem Delivered* is a fine example.

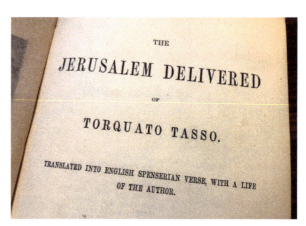

❦ Popular edition of *The Jerusalem Delivered* of Torquato Tasso, translated by J. H. Wiffen

Tasso, the brilliant poet, was a creative genius whose greatest pleasures were study and writing. At the same time he suffered deeply from mental illness,

CHAPTER 5: THE EPIC POET

with episodes of depression and mania, which today is considered to have been bipolar disorder. Tasso's time in Ferrara illustrates his struggles over mental health. In 1579, he joined the court of Alfonso d'Este, the Duke of Ferrara. There Tasso—in good times—penned the first version of his masterpiece, *Jerusalem Delivered*. Later, he found himself frustrated with the conditions at the court, feeling under-appreciated by his patrons and envied by his colleagues. This was a fatal combination for Tasso, who was already psychologically unstable and is said to have developed a persecution complex that led to a fit of violence the same year. That breakdown led him to being imprisoned in a convent, from which he later escaped. He was then confined to a madhouse, where he remained until his release in 1586, after seven years in captivity.

Torn and harassed with delirium and in constantly declining health, Tasso arrived in Rome for the last time on November 10, 1594.[3] There he was met by a splendid cavalcade and brought to the Vatican to see the pope. The following day he was granted an audience with Clement VIII, who praised him for his genius. When Clement had been elected to the See of Peter, Tasso celebrated the election with a poem he wrote for the occasion, which soon led to an invitation to the Vatican from the pope himself. The pope said to him at this final meeting between the two, "We have destined you the crown of laurel, that from you it may receive as much honor, as since times past it has conferred on others."[4] The pope then gave him a munificent gift in the form of a generous sum of money, a pension, proof of the admiration and esteem the Holy Father had for the renowned poet.

[3]. Over the years, when Tasso would visit Rome, he stayed at different locations. In Rome's Via della Scrofa in the neighborhood of Campo Marzio, there is a marble plaque placed on the side of a palace by the Comune di Roma, commemorating that Tasso stayed there at the home of Cardinal Scipione Gonzaga various times between the years 1587 and 1590.

[4]. J. H. Wiffen, *The Jerusalem Delivered: A Life of the Author*, 53.

PART II: THE MONASTERY AND ITS PERSONAGES

By spring, Tasso's health had deteriorated considerably due to an aggravation of his disorders. Tasso was given shelter at the monastery of Sant'Onofrio because the air was praised by physicians as the best in Rome and also because he desired to be at this exalted place, amid the seclusion and care of the devout monks. Permission for him to stay in the monastery was secured through the one man who was perhaps his best friend, Cardinal Cinzio Aldobrandini (1551–1610), nephew of the pope. Tasso, with great respect for his eminent friend the cardinal, had dedicated his *Gerusalemme Conquista* to him several years before. Tasso arrived at the monastery in the cardinal's private coach on a stormy and rainy day on April 1, 1595. As the monks came to the carriage to greet him, Tasso stepped out and spoke to the prior, saying he had come to die with him.

Days later, finding himself more feeble than ever, Tasso wrote a letter to an old friend of his, "What will my dear Constantini say when he shall hear of the death of his dear Tasso! And in my opinion, the tidings will not be tardy. The close of life I feel to be fast approaching; no remedy can be found to assuage this new distemper which has joined my others. So that, as by a rapid torrent, I am borne away, without any thing to cling to, or to oppose its speed. It avails not now to speak of my relentless fortune, nor to complain of the ingratitude of the world, which has gained the victory of conducting me indignant to the tomb, while I fondly hoped that the glory which (whatever it may think) this age shall derive from my writings, would not entirely leave me without reward. I have caused myself to be conducted into this Monastery of St. Onofrio, not only because the air of it is praised by the physicians as better than any in Rome, but also that I may begin at this exalted place, and with the intercourse of these devout friars, my conversation in Heaven."[5]

5. Ibid., 54.

Although Tasso was receiving the best medical care in the city, the end was near. A few days later, on April 10, he was seized with a violent fever. When death was near, he received the news without alarm, embracing the physician to thank him for news so agreeable. Raising his eyes to Heaven, he returned devout thanks to God after such an eventful and tempestuous life. Finally, he perceived he was being brought to a more calm haven. From this moment Tasso no longer spoke of terrestrial subjects but resigned himself wholly and with the liveliest devotion to the last solemn moments of his life. The poet made a good Confession with great contrition and received the Blessed Sacrament, with a reverence and humility that affected all who were present.

At this point, seeing the final hour was near, Cardinal Aldobrandini requested from his uncle the pope the Apostolic Pardon, which was readily granted to Tasso. The pope is said to have groaned and sighed over the news of the fate of so great a talent. He granted the blessing with a plenary indulgence for the remission of the temporal punishment due to his sins. Tasso acknowledged this with "humility and gratitude, saying, this was the chariot upon which he hoped to go crowned, not with laurel as a poet into the capitol, but with glory as a saint to Heaven."[6]

6. Ibid., 55.

When Tasso was requested to dictate a will and to offer some poetic words as an epitaph, he smiled and said that he had little to leave and a plain stone would be sufficient to cover his tomb. He nevertheless asked his confessor to write down that he bequeathed to the nobleman

Manso his portrait, which had been painted on his direction, and to Cardinal Aldobrandini his personal writings along with his few items of personal property. He further begged the cardinal to collect together all the copies of his works and especially of the *Gerusalemme* and to commit them to the flames. The cardinal, unwilling to embitter the final moments of his friend, avoided a direct refusal, and Tasso was satisfied. In any event, the cardinal knew it was out of his power to fulfill such an impossible request.

After Tasso had obtained all that he could possibly wish for in this world, he asked to be left alone with a crucifix in his room on the second floor of the monastery. One or two of the monks remained in his room to assist him with his palliative care and last devotions. His last outside visitor was Cardinal Aldobrandini, who bade his old friend a final farewell and left the room in tears. After this, no one was admitted to the room except his confessor and a few of the fathers. The monks took turns taking care of the dying man while singing Psalms and praying the prayers for the sick and dying in an audible voice, occasionally joined by Tasso himself until his voice failed. Even then, Tasso steadily contemplated the image of his Redeemer on the crucifix. At the very end, he closely embraced the same crucifix and uttered his last recorded words, "Into Thy hands, O Lord," as he resigned his peaceful spirit, dying at eleven o'clock in the morning on April 25, 1595. Thus, a peaceful end to a most eventful life. Tasso was fifty-one.

In death, the newly deceased poet was dressed in a Roman toga and crowned with laurels. That same day, his corpse was exposed for public viewing and afterwards borne in state

CHAPTER 5: THE EPIC POET

by a massive torchlight procession through the principal streets of Rome. Crowds flocked to catch one last glimpse of the famous poet. The evening of the very same day he died, Tasso was buried inside Sant'Onofrio (see Self-Guided Tour, 16), where he remains to this day.

ALTHOUGH TASSO'S WORKS historically have been widely read by Italian students in *liceo* (high school) up to today, and by English-speaking readers especially in the nineteenth century, he is not as well known as he was in previous generations. He certainly is deserving of more attention, at the least for his immense literary contributions.

Today, Italian school groups still flock to visit Tasso's final resting place at Sant'Onofrio. They also tour the room where he died in the adjoining monastery, converted into a museum dedicated to the poet (see Self-Guided Tour, 24). Some of them read a play in verse entitled *Torquato Tasso*, written by Johann Wolfgang von Goethe while he was in Italy (see Self-Guided Tour, 1). The play was completed in 1790 and found immediate success. It highlighted the descent into madness of the beloved poet and courtier.

In Italy and beyond, old stamps and commemorative coins depicting Tasso can be found in antique shops and in outdoor markets. A famous opera premiered in 1833 on the life of Tasso in three acts by Gaetano Donizetti. The libretto was written by Jacopo Ferretti, who created his text from various sources, including Goethe, Lord Byron, the playwright Carlo

Goldoni, and even Giovanni Rosini, who wrote a historic comedy on Tasso in 1832. Reminders of Tasso's fame are on display in the form of large outdoor statues seen in Italy, one in Sorrento (Piazza Torquato Tasso), the place of his birth, and another in Bergamo (Piazza Vecchia) in the north of Italy. A statue of his bust is on display in an outdoor park on Rome's Pincio promenade, realized in 1849–1852 by Filippo Gnaccarini.

Scenes from the poem *Jerusalem Liberated* became widely illustrated in art during the Baroque period. Italian and French painters depicted the love stories from the poem. Famous artists of the time, such as Poussin, Guercino, Turchi, Boucher and Tiepolo, were inspired by Tasso. For example, the artist Poussin was so touched by Tasso's poetic discourses that they became the most important source for his theory of painting. He even based his conception of narrative painting on Tasso's plot structure, artistic imitation, and unity, all exemplified by Tasso's *Jerusalem Liberated*.

Tasso's works were especially admired by Romantic era poets for his extraordinary imagery and the tragic fate of his life and demise. Lord Byron (1788–1824) authored *The Lament of Tasso* in 1817, a short dramatic monologue that describes Tasso's imprisonment in the madhouse. Lord Byron was so fascinated that he himself visited the cell where Tasso was kept during his stay in Italy. *Tasso in the Hospital of St. Anne at Ferrara*, a famous oil on canvas completed in 1839 by Eugene Delacroix (1811–1886), depicts Tasso during that unfortunate episode of his life. For Delacroix and others of his time, Tasso was the epitome of the artist-hero who suffered terribly for his art and beliefs.

CHAPTER 5: THE EPIC POET

Lastly, Franz Liszt, one of the greatest pianists of all time, composed in 1849 a symphonic poem entitled *Tasso: Lamento e Trionfo* (Tasso: Lament and Triumph). Liszt was drawn to Tasso's inner conflicts and his triumph over his sufferings after having read both Lord Byron and Goethe on the subject. The work by Liszt commemorates the seven years Tasso spent in an insane asylum at the hospital of St. Anne in Ferrara. In his preface to the work, Liszt refers to Goethe and Byron's works as his influence, both inviting his wonder and indignation at Tasso's captivity and illness.

Liszt's musical creation is a beautiful theme with cellos and double basses, presenting to the audience the drama of Tasso, complete with the poet's sufferings put to music with the melancholic sounds of a folk melody for bass clarinet, accompanied by strings and harps. The opening melody leads to the last section transformed into the proud and heroic sound of Tasso's final, ultimate triumph in Rome.

Liszt wrote in his preface, "Tasso loved and suffered at Ferrara. He was avenged at Rome. His glory still lives in the folk songs of Venice. These three elements are inseparable from his immortal memory. To represent them in music, we first called up his august spirit as he still haunts the waters of Venice. Then we beheld his proud and melancholy figure as he passed through the festivals of Ferrara, where he had produced his masterpieces. Finally we follow him to Rome, the Eternal City, which offered him the crown and glorified in him the martyr and the poet."[7]

7. Milton Cross and David Ewen. *Encyclopedia of the Great Composers and Their Music*, Volume I, 443.

PART II: THE MONASTERY AND ITS PERSONAGES

❡ Embossed image of Torquato Tasso on the cover of an antique edition of *The Jerusalem Delivered*

VARIOUS EDITIONS OF TASSO'S works in English and other languages are often seen in rare book collections. Collectors seek out richly illustrated and finely bound Victorian-era editions, some with features such as Morocco leather overlay covers and spines richly gilt with raised cords. Others display covers embossed and decorated in gilt with single fillet frames surrounded by floral sprays and corner fleurons. Special editions include bonus images made of engravings on wood or steel, while some have the rare quality of gilt page edges or fore-edge painting.

CHAPTER 5: THE EPIC POET

The most famous translation into English of Tasso's greatest work is entitled *The Jerusalem Delivered*, translated by J. H. Wiffen in the mid-1800s. This colorful translation is in Spenserian stanza, a fixed verse that is song to the ears. This translation went through multiple editions in both England and the United States.

✣

☫ Collectible edition of Tasso's *The Jerusalem Delivered*

TASSO, THE ILLUSTRIOUS POET and the greatest bard of the conquest of Jerusalem, lives on through his works. There, in the profound silence that envelopes the chapel where he reposes at Sant'Onofrio (see Self-Guided Tour, 20), visitors enter in hushed silence and recite again the opening lines of his immortal poem in the first canto of *Jerusalem*

Delivered: "Cano l'arme pietose e 'l capitano che 'l gran sepolcro libero' di Cristo..." (Author's translation: *I sing the pious arms and captain, who freed the glorious sepulchre of Christ...*). The visitor pauses to hear the echo of heroic times, and for a few moments at least encounters the virtues and drama of the past, dimmed through the ages and made present for all who are led to Sant'Onofrio.

6
The Second Apostle of Rome

FOR CENTURIES, VISITors to Rome have followed in the footsteps of St. Philip Neri (1515–1595), who was very fond of visiting Sant'Onofrio. An immensely popular saint in Rome, he is called the Second Apostle of Rome due to his very successful evangelization efforts in the city. Pilgrims follow in his footsteps to see where the saint from Florence prayed, preached and reclined at Sant'Onofrio beneath the shadows of the oaks for his religious gatherings and conferences with young people.

Philip Neri took pleasure in the Church of Sant'Onofrio and would gather crowds there and preach from the portico. On the lawns of the gardens and orchards he would gather in open air with the Fathers of the Oratory he founded, and other young men who were being catechized. Neri was re-evangelizing Rome over the years of the early Counter-Reformation, "so that in the course of his long life the Roman Oratory became one of the great centers of the revival of religious life among the laity."[1]

Sant'Onofrio's former gardens on the brow of the hill mark the slope where St. Philip Neri so often came. Unfortunately, the original slope and vineyards were destroyed in the 1880's with the construction of the new road below, disrupting where Neri gathered his followers and taught them with great joy the splendors of Catholic culture. These meetings were held during the lifetime of Tasso as the two men were both

1. Christopher Dawson, *The Dividing of Christendom*, 187.

contemporaries. Although there is no account of Neri and Tasso actually meeting, that is not to say they didn't. Rome was small in those days. Tasso traveled to Rome various times and spent his final winter and spring there. We do know that St. Philip celebrated his last Mass with the particular intention of Tasso thirty days after his death, on May 25, 1595. This is known as a *trigesimo*, recorded in his Mass book, kept today at Rome's Chiesa Nuova.

With a little imagination, Neri and his followers can still be seen sitting there today in his memory on the Janiculum Hill, as the dying light of the late afternoon sun throws out on the city landscape the relief of a thousand beauties as the city is illuminated in the fading light of the day.

Neri's model of catechetical instruction mixed business with pleasure as he blended diversion and recreation with instruction in all things Catholic. Thus piety was rendered cheerful and attractive to all. In fact, the association Neri made of poetry and music and gladness with catechesis was a special feature of his wise and natural method. Indeed, St. Philip Neri, a friend of Palestrina and the new Baroque music, helped to usher in the beginnings of modern music as he is responsible for the institution of the *oratorio*, which was the ultimate ancestor of the Italian opera. The oratorio, by definition, was a musical work for an orchestra and voices that was typically a narrative on a religious theme, performed without the use of costumes or scenery or acting.

These meetings at Sant'Onofrio took place after Easter in the spring and summer months. In the autumn and winter months, they were held indoors at other locations. However, the gardens of Sant'Onofrio offered a matchless view of Rome, admirably fitted to enlist nature and art and imagination at the service of religion.

Neri began his meetings in the warmth of the late afternoon sun, after a brisk walk up the hill. The recitation of music, poetry and verse helped to open the hearts of the young to the grateful and joyous impressions of the good, true and beautiful. Good conversation and authentic sacred and folk music were staples of the experience. The gatherings consisted of exhortations and spiritual exercises, sermons and short conferences on religion. The group would begin their meeting with a devout hymn. Then a boy would recite a short sermon he had memorized previously. Next there would be another song and some music. Then one of the Fathers of the Oratory would deliver a discourse, followed by more music and song. The encounter was intended to be a bright and glad feast where the thoughts of God were blended with rest and relaxation while the listeners connected with the beauty of nature and Catholic culture.

This practice of moving his Oratory outside to the cool spot of a garden for sermons and musical interludes proved the genius of Neri's psychology of education. Accompanied by his Oratorians and large crowds, in those years before Rome was built up, the panorama of the city was more spectacular than ever as the city spread out like a stage below. The backdrop of the Alban and Sabine Hills was epic with clear views of the Castel Sant'Angelo. Dominant in the religious exercises was a buoyant recreational tone that was set by Neri himself. Needless to say, Sant'Onofrio's vineyard on the slope remained

PART II: THE MONASTERY AND ITS PERSONAGES

one of Neri's favorite places until his death. In 1590, for the first time, the Oratorians rented the slope on the Janiculum directly from the monastery for this very purpose. The guarantor was Prince Fabrizio dei Massimi, one of the benefactors of the Oratorians. The whole setting provided a perfect theatre, a place for undisturbed conversation and song. While Neri enjoyed a crowd with the spiritual nurturing of young men singing and learning together, he also enjoyed climbing alone to the highest point of the hill to pray in silence.

❰ Sketch of the old gardens of Sant'Onofrio since destroyed by urban development

✠

ALTHOUGH VERY DIFFERENT from each other, Neri and Tasso are linked forever by their connection with Sant'Onofrio. They died a month apart: Tasso on April 25 at Sant'Onofrio and Neri on May 26 at the nearby Chiesa Nuova. Only after Neri died was his Congregation able to purchase the

CHAPTER 6: THE SECOND APOSTLE OF ROME

slope on the Janiculum to continue his tradition of gathering permanently at this site. In 1619 the Oratorians built there an outdoor theatre on the slope next to Tasso's oak. Under this oak tree is where legend averred Tasso had reclined reciting poetry, resting against the gentle hollow on the hillside, a story considered feasible by many—the dead tree is still visible today.

Converting the natural slope into a permanent and graceful place of meetings proved a wise move, and for over two hundred years followers of Neri and lovers of Tasso's poetry gathered at this spot until the nineteenth century, a time of revolution and change in the city of Rome. The old holm oak named after Tasso was struck by lightning on September 22, 1843, breaking off all the branches except one. Meanwhile, the tree was left still standing, in a decrepit state. Later in the century the theatre built by the Oratorians was expropriated by the State while the passage was transformed into a new walkway for the public.

Today, visitors can still be seen following the Tasso-Neri trail, which leads to the venerable holm oak, still standing at the far end of the old monastery vineyard, just south of the monastery. The grassy footpath is called the Rampa di Quercia, where the road bends to the right behind the monastery. Poets and hymnodists can be seen gathering here to recite Tasso's poetry and reflect on everyday life and the evangelization of Rome and the life and mission of St. Philip Neri.

What is left of the dead tree can be seen today held up by a brick buttress with ironwork supporting its base and branches. On the front of the buttress is a commemorative plaque

PART II: THE MONASTERY AND ITS PERSONAGES

2. Robin Anderson, *Rome Churches of Special Interest for English-Speaking People*, 59.

dedicated in 1898. Quoting the words of the plaque, English historian Robin Anderson reflects on Tasso and Neri under the same tree, "The poet used to meditate in its shade upon 'all the miseries of life' (so the inscription reads); whilst a contemporary of his, St. Philip Neri, on this same spot, 'wisely made himself a child with children amid joyful cries.'" ²

❦ Image of Tasso's oak as it looks today, with accompanying plaque dating from 1898

7
The Modern Friars

THE FRANCISCAN Friars of the Atonement of Graymoor in Garrison, New York, have been the official guardians and administrators of Sant'Onofrio since 1946.

These mostly American priests were invited by Venerable Pope Pius XII to take up residence in the monastery of Sant'Onofrio and to staff the church. While their role was envisioned by the pope to satisfy the needs of those who came to see the church and to worship, he also intended for them to have the added role of assisting at the altar for the religious services and ceremonies of the Equestrian Order of the Holy Sepulchre, an order of knighthood of which Sant'Onofrio is their official Roman home. The Society of the Atonement consists not only of friars, but also of sisters, known together as the Graymoor Friars and Sisters. These religious are dedicated to promoting Christian unity, with special devotion to the Blessed Mother under the title of Our Lady of Atonement.

The new community has a unique history in that it was originally not a Catholic society. It was founded in 1898 in New York by an Episcopalian minister, Paul Wattson, SA. On October 30, 1909, both the men's and women's societies were received into full communion with the Catholic Church. The unprecedented step of welcoming all seventeen members of the society into the Church as a religious order was through the good graces of Pope St. Pius X on the advice of his Cardinal Secretary of State, Rafael Merry del Val. For the past several decades these Franciscan friars have kept the church and monastery going, faithfully offering daily Mass and sacraments to all who visit. Although as a religious order, they near their terminal stage due to a dearth of vocations, we pray for the next chapter that an order worthy of the charge and living anew the traditions of the past may assume the responsibility to bring new life and leadership to this great community, a citadel of faith.

PART III
A Global Chivalric Movement

℄ Rendition of trophy of the Equestrian
Order of the Holy Sepulchre,
fresco from Sant'Onofrio

8
History and Mission of the Equestrian Order

THE CHURCH'S UNIversality is seen and felt as nowhere else in the city of Rome. Sant'Onofrio's has been designated by the Holy See as the official church in Rome of the Equestrian Order of the Holy Sepulchre of Jerusalem (EOHSJ), in Latin: *Ordo Equestris Sancti Sepulchri Hierosolymitani*. This is a Catholic order of knighthood that still exists today under the protection of the Holy See, one which originated at the time of the First Crusade. "In the annals of chivalry there is no more glorious chapter than the story of the Equestrian Order of the Holy Sepulchre of Jerusalem, a Knighthood that is one of the oldest of its kind. Not started as a reward of merit, it had men come from all of Europe to try to join its ranks for a great purpose—service; service in arms to preserve the cradle of Christianity, Jerusalem the beloved and the Tomb of Our Lord; and service to the greatest of all Kings, Jesus Christ."[1]

THE HISTORICAL ORIGIN OF THE Order can be traced back to the year 1099, when the Holy Sepulchre was delivered during the First Crusade. The first organized body of the knights appeared at that time under

1. Michael H. Abraham D'Assemani, *The Cross on the Sword*, from the Preface. This book, by the man who was once the official representative in America of the Latin Patriarch of Jerusalem, is the best history of the Order in English.

PART III: A GLOBAL CHIVALRIC MOVEMENT

Sir Godfrey of Bouillon, the first *princeps* (ruler) of the Kingdom of Jerusalem and *advocatus* (defender, protector) of the Holy Sepulchre of Christ. The motto of the Order is *Deus Lo Vult* (God Wills It).

The roots of the Order and the concept of the virtue of chivalry remain tied to the Crusades. Chivalry is a name for that general spirit or state of mind which disposes men to heroic and generous actions, keeping them conversant with all that is great and sublime in the moral and intellectual spheres. The motto of the brave Louis, husband of St. Elizabeth of Hungary, was that of all chivalry: *Pie, Caste, Juste* (Godly, Chastely, Justly). Catholic historians agree that the First Crusade, which was fought from 1096 to 1099, ushered in a new epoch of brave knighthood and noble chivalry. "The high point in the age of chivalry came during the Crusades, those religious wars waged in the twelfth and thirteenth centuries by the Christians of Western Europe against the Mohammedans for the recovery of the Holy Land. An interaction came about between the Crusades and chivalry. The spirit of chivalry was largely responsible for making possible these campaigns for a religious ideal. Thereby, the Crusades provided a powerful impetus in the development of knighthood, for it was during the twelfth and thirteenth centuries that chivalry attained its highest peak both in quality and quantity. The Crusades did not create a new type of knighthood, but they gave the knights a chance to show their mettle."[2]

The first Knights of the Order spent their lives guarding the newly liberated tomb of Christ. The Order received papal approbation from Pope Pascal II in 1113.

2. James Van der Veldt, O. F. M., *The Ecclesiastical Orders of Knighthood*, 6–7.

CHAPTER 8: HISTORY AND MISSION OF THE EQUESTRIAN ORDER

The EOHSJ is today described as an order of chivalry within the Church, salvaging noble values from the past — a symbolic combination of all the qualities of an ideal knight. In the admirable and very interesting book of chivalrous instruction by Gilles of Rome entitled *The Mirror*, it is laid down how the prince, baron, or knight "should be grounded in the truth of faith, steadfast in the faith, firm in hope, firm in the love of God, perfect in the fear of God, 'he ought to be fervent in prayer for the love of Jesus Christ; to have reverence and devotion towards the Church; to be humble in himself; to have reasonable knowledge; to be stable in perseverance; and constant in execution; honest in conversation, secret in consultation, discreet in speech, courteous in receiving strangers, liberal in gifts, magnificent and noble in actions, magnanimous in enterprises, continent in purity, abstinent in sobriety, amiable in all good qualities, incomparable in clemency, and invincible in patience.'"[3]

Knights of today no longer stand in steel breastplate, military tunic, plated gauntlets and a sufficient weight of armor with sword and triangular shield. Instead, the accoutrements of modern knighthood are today the great values and ideals of the past. Catholic commentaries on the subject expound the role of chivalry in the context of Catholic knighthood and the values espoused by it: "Hardly an institution in the world today has the equivalent of honors parallel to that of the Roman Catholic Church. In an age when initiative and ability tend to become lost in the overwhelming social changes that are so universal, these honors stand out as another instance of the timelessness of that Church. They salvage values and ideals from the past. Chivalry is more

3. Kenelm Henry Digby, *The Broad Stone of Honour: Or the True Sense and Practice of Chivalry.* Tancredus, 49–50.

than romance; it is one of the graces of human dignity. Those who would spurn the past cannot build the future. These honors are enshrined in a morality and code that is rooted in the love and charity of Christ made visible through human compassion and effort. They envision the kingdom of Heaven as their perspective quite in the way of the parable Our Lord so earnestly preached when He tenderly uttered the words: 'Well done, good and faithful servant.'" [4]

The concept of chivalry, familiar in the medieval period, was based on a unity of outlook that united a medieval king such as St. Louis IX with the humblest of his subjects, or the medieval noble with the guild craftsman, despite the difference in social status. Chivalry fell into decline during the Renaissance in part because of the new era's ideals of life, and education was rapidly developing from the recovery of classical learning and Greek culture. In the humanist circles that were developing, a new ideal of culture was based on the harmonious development of body and mind in all their activities. "Such "universal men," as Leon Battista Alberti, at once athlete and scholar, architect and poet, artist and scientist, were a characteristic product of fifteenth-century Italy, and it was this new type of many-sided excellence which took the place of the medieval ideals of chivalry, as the model of the European gentleman and courtier in the following age. In the Renaissance, there was a shift in culture. Life was no longer seen as a struggle and a pilgrimage as in the Middle Ages. Instead, it came to be seen as a fine art, in which no opportunity for knowledge or enjoyment was meant to be neglected."[5]

4. Van der Veldt, *The Ecclesiastical Orders of Knighthood*, 54.

5. Christopher Dawson, *The Dividing of Christendom*, 62.

CHAPTER 8: HISTORY AND MISSION OF THE EQUESTRIAN ORDER

THE PRIMARY MISSION TODAY of the EOHSJ is to support the Christian presence in the Holy Land. Churches, convents, seminaries and schools in and around Jerusalem are supported by the Order, including forty-five schools under the jurisdiction of the Roman Catholic Bishop of Jerusalem (also known as the Latin Patriarchate) with close to twenty thousand students.

The Order is, at the same time, one of the oldest and yet one of the least-known organizations within the Catholic Church. Today, the EOHSJ has an estimated thirty thousand members, with sixty lieutenancies around the world, and growing. The Pope is the Sovereign of the Order, while the Grand Master is a Cardinal in Rome, and the Grand Prior is the Latin Patriarch of Jerusalem.

The Order has had the unique task in history of having been chosen to guard the most sacred locale in all Christendom — the empty tomb of Christ in Jerusalem. Indeed, it can be said that "Every country has a soul, Palestine a profound one — the tomb of the Redeemer of the human race. It is the most hallowed spot in all the world — a spot respected and revered."[6]

The Order is zealous for fostering holiness and the preservation and spread of the faith in the Holy Land. The Holy See has given a two-fold modern mission to the members of the Order: to foster the practice of the Christian life in the world at large and to preserve the faith in the Holy Land, forever the birthplace of Christianity.

[6]. D'Assemani, *The Cross on the Sword*, 19.

PART III: A GLOBAL CHIVALRIC MOVEMENT

The EOHSJ supports and furthers the missions of the Latin Patriarchate of Jerusalem, giving assistance to its good works and to its charitable, cultural and social undertakings. At the same time, it champions the defense and rights of the Catholic Church in its ecclesiastical jurisdiction, which includes Israel, Palestine, Jordan and Cyprus. All members are encouraged to make at least one pilgrimage in their lifetimes to the Holy Land, to walk in the footsteps of Jesus and see the empty tomb of Christ, and return home as first-hand eyewitnesses and ambassadors of Christ.

Members pray daily for the Holy Land and strive to be witnesses of Christ, with special ties to the holy city of Jerusalem, bringing to mind Jesus' declaration to the apostles: "But you shall receive the power of the Holy Ghost coming upon you, and you shall be witnesses unto me in Jerusalem, and in all of Judea, and Samaria, and even to the uttermost part of the earth" (Acts 1:8 Douay–Rheims).

MEMBERSHIP IN THE EOHSJ is by invitation only. Only practicing Catholics who are serious about their faith are admitted for membership, after being sponsored by members and approved by their pastor, bishop, and the Holy See. Often when an individual is invited to accept membership in the Order, the question arises: Why me? Selection occurs because of meritorious service to the Church, to the community and to one's fellow man. Frequently this is not obvious to the

CHAPTER 8: HISTORY AND MISSION OF THE EQUESTRIAN ORDER

individual nominated. The honor is bestowed upon the person who has demonstrated fidelity, with notable professional accomplishments and readiness to serve the Church.

Members are accorded a high station in the Church while membership is considered one of the highest honors conferred upon clergy and laity alike. In addition to being an honor, membership carries certain spiritual and temporal responsibilities, first among which is daily prayer for the Christians in the Holy Land. Members are also expected to give in a spirit of largesse to help promote the religious and charitable works of the Latin Patriarchate in Jerusalem.

It can be said, "The religious character of the knightly Order of the Holy Sepulchre comes to the fore not only in the description of its objective and the required qualifications of its members, but also in the ceremonial investiture of the newly elected knights which was approved by the Congregation of Sacred Rites, Aug. 24, 1945.[7] This ceremony combines a profession of faith with the ancient ritual used for the dubbing of knighthood. The candidates do not take monastic vows but promise to live an upright Christian life in accordance with the commandments of God and the precepts of the Church, in absolute fidelity to the Supreme Pontiff, as true soldiers of Christ."[8]

The annual investitures for the Lieutenancy of Central Italy are held at the Lateran Archbasilica. The rituals of the Order are a sight to behold, including the ancient ritual used for the dubbing of knights, evocative of the age of faith. This brings to mind the importance of ritual in relation to human nature and membership in

---

7. Please note, the rite has since been updated.

8. Van der Veldt, *The Ecclesiastical Orders of Knighthood*, 40.

the Order: "In every great religion, ritual is as necessary as creed. It instructs, nourishes, and often begets belief; it brings the believer into comforting contact with his God; it charms the senses and soul with drama, poetry and art; it binds individuals into a fellowship and a community by persuading them to share in the same rites, the same prayers, at last the same thoughts."[9]

Knights of the Order continue their work and presence in Rome, considering themselves as direct heirs in perpetual emanation of the first knights while adapting themselves to the exigency of modern times. Meanwhile, the religious fervor of the Order continues strongly, bringing to mind a quotation of His Beatitude Luigi Barlassina, Patriarch of Jerusalem (1920–1947), "the noble religious fervor which spurred Godfrey to many a victory and inspired Tasso to write the heroic poem, *Jerusalem Delivered*, remains unchanged."[10]

9. Will Durant, *The Story of Civilization*, Vol. IV (The Age of Faith), 230.

10. John Pane-Gasser, Official Investiture Program, 3.

9
The Order's Spiritual Center in Rome

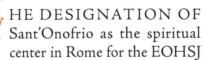HE DESIGNATION OF Sant'Onofrio as the spiritual center in Rome for the EOHSJ was given by Venerable Pope Pius XII on August 15, 1945. This was in response to the growing needs of the Order, which would go on to expand in the postwar years, especially in the United States. With his *motu proprio*, Pope Pius XII sought to grant to the Order the use

❡ Venerable Pius XII (1958)

of the Church of Sant'Onofrio together with the adjoining monastery and Torquato Tasso Museum for perpetuity. This would include the *magni cineres*, the great ashes of the poet Tasso, entombed in the side chapel of the church.

Having Sant'Onofrio's for the Order proved a tremendous grace, as a convenient center in Rome for the carrying out of religious ceremonies and various works of piety and charity. The specific reason given by the pope was that since the EOHSJ did not have its own Roman church, he desired to grant it one which would be not only proof of his benevolence toward the Order, but also one that would be especially fitting and have a particular significance for the Order's members. Needless to say, the tomb of Tasso played a big part, as well as the location, near to the Vatican and a short walk from the Palazzo della Rovere, a late fifteenth-century palace that once belonged to Cardinal Domenico Rovere, which is today the administrative headquarters of the Grand Magisterium of the Order.

In 1946, extensive repairs and improvements were made by the Knights and Dames to bring the old church, cloister and convent of Sant'Onofrio back to its original glory. The best minds and artists of the time in the Vatican were brought in to help with the project. "The order considered it a sacred trust confided to it to restore and repair the edifice that was to be their own special shrine. The services of qualified artistry and artisans were sought under the chief Architect of the Sacred Apostolic Palaces, Count Enrico Pietro Galeazzi [1896–1986] who was also the leading layman of the order. The entire interior of the church was restored to its former splendor. Stained glass windows bearing the coat-of-arms of the Order replaced the old ones. Richly carved benches of stained oak took the place of wicker chairs and kneelers. In the choir loft alterations were made to provide a place of prayer for the religious community to whom the care and functioning of the church were later to be entrusted [...] the church continues to be considered among the most beautiful and most interesting of the smaller churches in Rome."[1]

This effort was also assisted by Cardinal Nicola Canali (1874–1961), an Italian prelate who, in those days, was the Cardinal Protector of the Order. Canali, who was from a noble family of the hereditary rank of marquis, had devoted his energies and position of influence for many years to support the Order. The cardinal had a storied career in the Vatican, where in 1903 he became secretary to Cardinal Merry del Val, who was a close collaborator of Pope St. Pius X and, later, his Secretary of State. Canali and Merry del Val became lifelong friends, supporting the Order in many ways. Canali was created cardinal in 1935 and held various roles in the service of the Holy See, while never consecrated bishop (something that is sometimes done, as in the case of Cardinal Avery Dulles, S. J.). Cardinal Canali was made Protector of the EOHSJ on July 16, 1940, and was made its Grand Master on December 26, 1949. He held this title until his death in 1961 at age eighty-seven. The cardinal is buried in a side chapel of Sant'Onofrio, the church that he was so fond of and worked so hard to restore and maintain as a special place in Rome for all members of the EOHSJ.

It was during the postwar renovation and continued updating that the interior was slightly refashioned in a few places to suit the exigencies

[1] Sir Alfred J. Blasco, *The Modern Crusaders*, 70–71.

PART III: A GLOBAL CHIVALRIC MOVEMENT

of the new occupants. This included various updates to the adjoining convent and the tasteful addition of various emblems of the Order to the church interior in those early years to make it official. Alterations included some fresco and marble works, as well as an altar, tomb and stained-glass windows depicting the official emblem of the Order, the Jerusalem Cross, also known as the Crusader Cross.

Visitors to Sant'Onofrio are welcomed by this cross and see it multiple times inside and outside the church. Its symbolism holds great weight for members of the Order. The crest consists of the depiction of five potent red

❧ Rendition of the crest of the Equestrian Order of the Holy Sepulchre, taken from Sant'Onofrio

crosses, arranged as a large cross surrounded by four smaller crosslets. This crest is recognized all through the Holy Land and beyond. The statutes of the Order have designated the emblem as the special insignia for members of the EOHSJ and of the Latin Patriarchate of Jerusalem. The emblem honors the passion of Christ: the crosses represent the five sacred wounds of Christ in the hands, feet, and side of Our Blessed Lord.

One of the side chapels of Sant'Onofrio was refurbished and rededicated in the 1950s to Pope St. Pius X, Grand Master of the Order from 1907–1914. It includes an altarpiece painting of the newly canonized saint by Guido Greganti, completed in 1957. A few years earlier during the renovation completed in 1947, the inner cloister was restored, bringing back the original look to the upper loggia of the cloister, which had previously been enclosed some years before. This substantial restoration project brought the cloister into harmony with the church building, revealing the original effect intended by the artist who had designed it.

The Knights and Dames of the Order of the Holy Sepulchre are reminded that Sant'Onofrio is forever their spiritual home in Rome — their own special church practically in the shadow of the Vatican. Indeed, the cupola of St. Peter's can be seen from the attached convent and gardens, where colorful oleanders, magnolias and rhododendrons have bloomed over the years.

10
Pope Pius XII's Motu Proprio

THE ACT DATED AUGUST 15, 1945, in which His Holiness Pope Pius XII designated the church and monastery as the permanent spiritual home in Rome of the EOHSJ, follows here in an English translation:[1]

1. Frank Folsom, *Saint Onofrio on the Janiculum*, 11.

Motu Proprio

The use of the church dedicated to Saint Onofrio on the Janiculum Hill together with the adjoining monastery is granted to the Equestrian Order of the Holy Sepulchre of Jerusalem.

POPE PIUS XII

Since the Equestrian Order of the Holy Sepulchre of Jerusalem does not have its own church in the city of Rome, We desire to grant it one which may be not only proof of Our paternal benevolence toward the Order, but also one that may be especially fitting and have a particular significance for the same.

There is on the Janiculum Hill a splendid church dedicated to Saint Onofrio, distinguished since the sixteenth century with the honor of being a titular church of Cardinals belonging to the order of priests; this church appears to Us to be most suitable for realizing Our desire.

In this church, in fact, there still lives the memory of Torquato Tasso, illustrious poet, who sang in exquisite verse the deeds of the Crusaders who struggled to restore freedom to the Holy Sepulchre of Jerusalem: and there, too, is an ancient monastery, which — after the legitimate cessation of the Order of Hermits of St. Jerome — can fittingly accommodate this Equestrian Order and can provide it with a convenient center for the carrying out of its religious ceremonies and its acts of piety and works of charity.

Wherefore, after careful consideration of the matter, and having conferred with Our dearly beloved son Emanuel Celestine Suhard of the title of Saint Onofrio on the Janiculum, Cardinal Priest of the Holy Roman Church, Archbishop of Paris, by virtue of this *Motu Proprio*, with certain knowledge and by the fullness of Our Apostolic power, We decree and ordain as follows:

The use of the church dedicated to Saint Onofrio on the Janiculum Hill and likewise of the adjoining monastery and the Torquato Tasso Museum, with the furnishings and all the property both movable and those things fixed to the soil, which are called immovable, is assigned by law to the Equestrian Order of the Holy Sepulchre of Jerusalem;

The nomination of the Rector and of the other clergy to this church is the concern of the Sovereign Pontiff, having heard the judgment both of the Cardinal Priest of the title of Saint Onofrio on the Janiculum, and of the Most Eminent Cardinal Vicar of Rome, and of the Most Eminent Cardinal who is Patron of the Equestrian Order of the Holy Sepulchre of Jerusalem at the time;

This same church dedicated to Saint Onofrio shall likewise remain conveniently accessible in the future to all the faithful who may wish to frequent it from a motive of piety.

CHAPTER 10: POPE PIUS XII'S MOTU PROPRIO

All which We have decreed and ordained by this instrument, issued by *Motu Proprio*, shall be fixed and immutable, notwithstanding anything to the contrary, even be it worthy of very special regard.

Given at Rome, from St. Peter's, August 15, 1945, feast of the Assumption of the Virgin Mary, in the seventh year of Our Pontificate.

[Signed] Pius pp. XII

PART IV
Self-Guided Tour

☾ Antique engraving of Sant'Onofrio,
front elevation

11
Getting There

SANT'ONOFRIO IS located just southeast of the Vatican. It is best to arrive by foot because there is no place to park a car. The address is Piazza Sant'Onofrio. Its GPS coordinates are 41°53′50.1″ N 12°27′40.2″ E. Visitors can follow the Via del Gianicolo up from the Tiber River at Piazza della Rovere, walking past the Pontifical North American College on the right, and arriving at the church, which is located on the right next to the pediatric hospital named after the Baby Jesus.

Today, the church is regrettably open only in the mornings, an inconvenience for visiting groups keeping strict schedules.

The site is unfortunately inaccessible to visitors with restricted mobility.

Entrance to the museum (Self-Guided Tour, 24) is free of charge and has different hours. Visits are by appointment only on Tuesday afternoons from 4:00 pm to 6:00 pm. Admission is facilitated by volunteers. Interested persons are required to call ahead to book a visit. Student groups are especially welcome. The telephone number, which is subject to change, has been: 06 6877341.

THERE ARE TWO MASSES EVERY Sunday at Sant'Onofrio (except in August): 10:00 am and 12:00 pm. There currently is no daily Mass open to the public. The visiting hours for the church (Self-Guided Tour, 10) are Sunday to Friday from 9:00 am to 1:00 pm, and Saturday from 10:00 am to 1:00 pm. Visiting hours for the exterior cloister (Self-Guided Tour, 23), portico and courtyard are from 9:00 am to 6:30 pm (5:30 pm winter hours). The property is closed during the month of August, as well as for civic holidays, special feast days and events such as baptisms and weddings, and select community events of the friars.

Traditional days of visiting the church are not to be forgotten, as Pope Pius XI reminded the Catholic world of the importance of the habit and rhythm of the calendar of feasts, "People are instructed in the truths of faith and brought to appreciate the inner joys of religion far more effectively by the annual celebration of our sacred mysteries than by any official pronouncements of the Church."[1]

The traditional days follow below:

June 12, the feast of St. Onuphrius

July 25, the anniversary of the dedication of the church

September 29, the memorial of the founder of the monastery, Blessed Nicola da Forca Palena (a local feast)

October 25, feast of Our Lady of Palestine (customarily also transferred to the last Sunday in October).

In the past members of the EOHSJ have flocked to Sant'Onofrio on Holy Saturday to participate in the annual Easter Vigil, the highlight of the annual liturgical year for members of the Order.

1. The Liturgical Conference, *Mary in the Liturgy*, ix.

12
Map for Self-Guided Tour

❧ Map of Sant'Onofrio Church, Cloister and Monastery (Convent) with Museum

13
The Exterior Grounds

SANT'ONOFRIO HAS some important works of art and pictorial embellishments, both inside and out, made famous by their age, style and the artists who painted them. Structurally, the outside shines with its fifteenth-century Renaissance facade, an attempt to realize the classical ideal of harmony and proportion, the rhythmic unit of form and idea, of color and emotion in a living unity. The exterior of the building dates from the fifteenth century, with reconstructions done in the sixteenth through eighteenth centuries.

From the street, the church has an external identity continuous with the monastery complex. The narrow and small red brick *campanile* belfry that rises over the bottom left-hand corner of the rooftop nave identifies the building as a church. The tower rises from the roofline, with a few bells that clash and peal, announcing the hours of the day and prayer. The smallest bell is dedicated to Tasso. In 1849, the Janiculum was the site of military hostilities between the French army defending the pope and revolutionaries who were trying to seize the city of Rome from him during a short-lived Masonic Roman Republic. The story is told that Garibaldi, the general of the republican forces, came to Sant'Onofrio to claim the bells for them to be melted down for use as weapons and armaments. The prior of Sant'Onofrio, as the story goes, told him that one of the bells was ringing when Tasso died, causing Garibaldi to leave without confiscating the bells.

After a long walk up the hill to the church and midway up the front stairs, visitors pass through an iron gate installed in the 1940s, which displays the emblem of the EOHSJ, two Jerusalem Crosses, painted in red on a green metal fence.

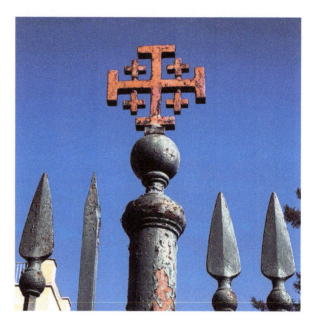

❡ The main entrance gate of Sant'Onofrio

As visitors arrive at the top of the stairs, they come to lovely outside gardens to the left, which were laid out in 1924 in memory of Tasso (Self-Guided Tour, 1). There, two stone benches provide a welcome place for a quiet respite for visitors after the ascent up the hill. The terrace here is famous for its *belvedere* panorama of the city of Rome. In previous generations, the view was even more incredible, as it is now partially blocked by buildings constructed in the late nineteenth and early twentieth centuries. Visitors are often seen resting in the small grassy

CHAPTER 13: THE EXTERIOR GROUNDS

courtyard while enjoying the splashing fountain with its shallow pool. Also present are a couple of remaining trees, a final reminder of the grand old holm oaks that once graced this hollow before the days of the monastery and urban development. The author hopes more oaks will be planted for posterity's sake.

❧ The fountain and garden of Sant'Onofrio

THE FOUNTAIN WAS ORIGINALLY put together from architectural salvage parts collected by the municipality of Rome at the end of the 1800s. Some of its parts had been taken from a famous fountain that was removed from Piazza Giudia in 1880. In 1930, the same fountain was restored as the *Fontana di Piazza della Cinque Scole* at a different location in Rome's neighborhood of the Jewish Ghetto. Meanwhile, the old fountain at the monastery was replaced with a simpler reproduction as a substitute, including a new bowl and baluster, carved of travertine in much simpler design.

83

PART IV: SELF-GUIDED TOUR

To the left of the main portico entrance, on the outer walls of the Chapel of St. Jerome, are found five stone plaques that commemorate various personages (Self-Guided Tour, 2). They include such eminent churchmen as Cardinal Louis Frezza (1783–1837), the former titular cardinal-priest of Sant'Onofrio, and Cardinal Giuseppe Mezzofanti (1774–1849), a famous hyperpolyglot (see Self-Guided Tour, 17), as well as Francesco Patrizi (1529–1597), an Italian philosopher and scientist of Croatian descent (see Self-Guided Tour, 20), all of whom are buried inside the church. Other inscriptions on the plaques are in memory of visits to Sant'Onofrio by important figures. One of these, placed under the short arm of the loggia most recently in 2003, commemorates Johann Wolfgang von Goethe, who while in Italy wrote a play about the life of Tasso and came to visit his tomb in 1787. Another plaque commemorating François-René de Chateaubriand (1768–1848), a French writer, politician and diplomat, who came in homage to the tomb of Tasso in 1828 while he was ambassador to Rome, was placed under the loggia in 1948 to mark the centenary of his passing.

14
The Renaissance Loggia

IN A CITY LIKE ROME, UNIversal principles of composition are always at work in the area of architectural aesthetic. This includes canons of objective beauty, reflected first in the exterior view. The forms of the Renaissance orders are easily recognizable, studied and learned by architects and art enthusiasts from the treatises of greats, such as Vitruvius, Alberti, Serlio, Vignola and others, who envisioned function to follow form. These master builders laid the foundation and rules for the systematic design, combination and ornamentation of typical Renaissance buildings in Rome. Symmetry and harmony, ornament, mass and execution were taken into careful consideration. The finished product is a timeless way to build according to universal and intuitively understood principles of beauty. The classical theory of the orders shines at Sant'Onofrio with the entrance loggia seen from the exterior front (Self-Guided Tour, 3).

THE OUTSIDE ENTRANCE TO the church is enclosed on two sides by a sixteenth-century entrance loggia with arches, created also with ancient columns that are obvious architectural salvage from ancient Rome, finished with simple Doric capitals

(Self-Guided Tour, 9). The ceiling of the loggia is cross-vaulted with white plaster and is presently undecorated. This front loggia is L-shaped and two stories, with the main level being in the open air. Its short arm is along the front of the church and its long arm is situated on the right, along the front of the monastery. There are four arches in the short end, containing the church entrance with nine arches in the long end, containing the entrance to the monastery and cloister. The arches encase eight columns of different sizes and colors. Five are grey granite, one in grey marble, and two in *marmo imezio*, a rare marble from Greece.

❰ Front portico of Sant'Onofrio, with flag of the Equestrian Order of the Holy Sepulchre

As the community of monks at Sant' Onofrio expanded over the years with new members, the need arose for extra space, especially for rooms on the upper level. Some time at the start of the eighteenth century, the two arches on the left-hand side of the loggia in front of the church on the main level were intentionally walled up, so as to create a porter's room next to the church entrance. In many

CHAPTER *14*: THE RENAISSANCE LOGGIA

ways, this was an unfortunate move, due to the change in the now disturbed front view of the church. It was during the same restoration that the arched, arcaded, second-story gallery of the portico was also walled up to enlarge the living quarters of the monastery on the upper level, as well as the choir loft in the church. The arches were then covered and replaced with stucco squaring.

Under the covered loggia at the end of the long arm is a little chapel called the Cappella Vaini (Self-Guided Tour, 4), also known as the Chapel of the Rosary. The chapel was fitted out in 1620 for Guido Vaini, the prince of Cantalupo. In order to do this, two arches had to be walled up at the end of the long arm of the loggia. The family crest depicting a lion can be seen above the entrance door of the chapel.

The outdoor lunette above depicts two sibyls, attributed by some to Agostino Tassi (1578–1644).[1] The sibyls were pagan oracles of the ancient world, women who according to legend prophesied on various subjects, their oracles notoriously open to interpretation. Some of the sibylline prophesies, it is said, were read to the Emperor Augustus, warning him of the advent of the coming of Christ, as they were influenced by spirits of the netherworld who knew the Incarnation was imminent.

Tassi's sibyls clearly mimic the sibyls of the Sistine Chapel, painted by Michelangelo decades before, between 1508 and 1512. This is

1. Tassi is often remembered as a sordid character, who, in 1611, raped the young Artemisia Gentileschi (1593–1656), a renowned female artist of the time, who was spectacularly successful in later life and testified against him in a seven-month rape trial.

seen most clearly in the calibrated musculature of the female bodies, the simple result of having male only models, the typical custom of that time.

Despite his notoriously low character, Tassi enjoyed some renown in his day as a painter of illusionistic architectural decoration and perspective, something very popular in the age after Michelangelo. In fact, the influence of the Sistine Chapel on Tassi and other painters of the High Renaissance cannot be overstated.

The two richly decorated outdoor inscriptions on the right recall the establishment of a daily Mass in the chapel; and on the left, the granting of indulgences of Santa Maria Sopra Minerva by Cardinal Maffeo Barberini (the future Pope Urban VIII), the titular Cardinal of Sant'Onofrio from 1620 to 1623. On the floor of the porch just beyond the chapel is the tombstone of the Salandra family, likely benefactors of the community.

Though the chapel is usually closed, it is sometimes accessible by speaking with the porter of Sant'Onofrio, who is generally to be found in the sacristy (Self-Guided Tour, 15). Art historians and other visitors are eager for the chapel to one day be open daily for those who may wish to visit and pray. The interior is Baroque in design and is also attributed to Tassi. The altarpiece is a rendition of the Nativity of Our Lord by Francesco Bassano the Younger (1549–1592).

CHAPTER 14: *THE RENAISSANCE LOGGIA*

❧ Fresco details of front portico of Sant'Onofrio

THE MAIN ATTRACTION ON THE outside front is a set of three outdoor lunettes on the long arm of the loggia seen on the side of the front wall of the monastery (Self-Guided Tour, 5). These are early works by the Baroque painter Domenico Zampieri (1581–1641), known by the diminutive Domenichino, which he painted between 1604 and 1605, showcasing scenes from the life of St. Jerome in commemoration of the hermits who lived on site. They include, from left to right, *The Baptism*, *The Vision* and *The Temptation*. *The Vision* involves the playful story of Christ telling an angel to give Jerome a beating for being overly fond of reading Cicero, a secular author.

PART IV: SELF-GUIDED TOUR

❦ The monumental door in the portico that leads to the atrium and cloister of Sant'Onofrio.

On the long side of the porch above the door that leads into the atrium (Self-Guided Tour, 22) and cloister (Self-Guided Tour, 23), a monumental neoclassical travertine stone frame around the door was erected in 1602 by the Madruzzo family, in memory of Blessed Pietro Gambacorti, co-founder of the Congregation of St. Jerome (Self-Guided Tour, 6).

CHAPTER 14: THE RENAISSANCE LOGGIA

❦ Detail of original tomb of Blessed Nicola da Forca Palena, outside entrance of Sant'Onofrio

ON THE WALL TO THE RIGHT of the main portico entrance of the church, catching the eye of every visitor, is the original tombstone of Blessed Nicola da Forca Palena (1349–1449), the monk who founded Sant'Onofrio (Self-Guided Tour, 7). The tombstone was moved here in 1712, when his remains were transferred from his original grave in the floor of the church to the main altar (Self-Guided Tour, 16), where they remain to this day. Pope Nicholas V, his friend in life, dictated the inscription. This tombstone is a masterpiece, the work of an unknown Tuscan sculptor in a style, art historians agree, similar to that of Donatello. Every line of the exquisitely carved image is worthy of attention. The head of the venerable hermit is cowled and rests on a cushion. His body is trapped in stone, yet his face is lifelike, befitting one asleep in the Lord.

CRESTS THAT DEPICT THE coat-of-arms of both the reigning Pontiff and Cardinal Protector of Sant'Onofrio can be seen displayed on the right and the left of the main entrance, respectively (Self-Guided Tour, 8). These cardinalatial crests are detachable and change with each new Pope that is elected and each new Cardinal Protector that is appointed to Sant'Onofrio. The current display is that of Cardinal Carlo Furno (1921–2015), a cardinal-priest who was once the Grand Master of the Equestrian Order of the Holy Sepulchre of Jerusalem. When the cardinal passed away in 2015 at age of ninety-four, Sant'Onofrio became vacant and will soon enough be given to a newly named cardinal-priest of the Holy Roman Church.

THE MAIN ENTRANCE TO THE church, also called the entrance portico, is framed with a white Carrara marble doorcase (Self-Guided Tour, 9). It has a large dedicatory inscription in Latin carved on its lintel: *Ecclesia S. Honuphrii* (Church of St. Onuphrius). The lunette above the door, attributed by most to Domenichino, depicts the Madonna and Child with Angels.

The composition seen above the door, today in poor condition, also includes two flanking lunettes on either side, believed to be perhaps by Sebastiano Strada. These depict various saints associated with the history and spirituality of the order of monks, venerating Our Lady with their names written beneath. They include, on the lunette above the right of the main church entrance, St. Augustine, St. Onuphrius, Blessed Nicolo da Forca Palena, Blessed Bartolomeo da Cesna, Marco da Mantova, Filippo da Folgaria and Giovanni da Catalonia, all praying before a crucifix. On the lunette above the left of the main entrance can be seen other saintly personages: St. Jerome, St. Paula and her daughter, Blessed Pietro Gambacorti da Pisa, Benedetto Siculo, Filippo di S. Agatha and Paolo Guerrini, all in prayer.

15
Interior Church and Chapels

THE CHURCH IS oriented north to south (Self-Guided Tour, 10). Like the exterior, the physical structure of the sanctuary dates from the mid-fifteenth century and, thankfully, updating the church has not significantly altered the original plan. Renaissance architecture was always built as a combination of the classical with a touch of innovation, with every artist eager to make his mark and outdo his predecessors. The Renaissance practice was to have a single nave, partly so that everyone in the congregation could see the altar. The main chapel of Sant'Onofrio is thus built with one nave only, which is rectangular, with three bays on each side and an external segmental apse in the sanctuary. The church is small. In fact, the floor area of the side chapels is greater than that of the church itself. The cross-vault ceiling above is plain and simple. The ceiling alone is a work of architectural design genius: two barrel vaults intersect at right angles, allowing a balance of immense weight to be held up with apparent ease.

The chapels along the side of the church are each like the rarest of flowers, of varying degrees of artistic merit according to their period and ornamentation, sharing a wealth of noteworthy works of art and design features. On the right-hand side of the church are two chapels, those of St. Onuphrius (Self-Guided Tour, 12) and Our Lady of Loreto (Self-Guided Tour,

13), followed by the sacristy (Self-Guided Tour, 15). On the left-hand side of the church there are three chapels: the Chapel of the Crucifix (Self-Guided Tour, 17), the Chapel of St. Pius X (Self-Guided Tour, 18) and the Chapel of St. Jerome (Self-Guided Tour, 19).

A PRAYER TO ST ONUPHRIUS

O most austere holy anchorite, St. Onuphrius, loving consoler of those in tribulation, diligent protector of the oppressed, effective relief of the wretched and abandoned, behold, humbly prostrate at thy feet, a poor sinner, deprived of the stole of innocence and divine grace through his innumerable faults and enormities, and for that reason weighed down with miseries and afflicted by grave tribulations, made the target of a thousand misfortunes, turns to thee, o most glorious St. Onuphrius, trusts in thee and asks for thy powerful aid. Thou who, in the sight of the Most High, swiftly grew with excellence of merits so extraordinary that you obtained for those devoted to thee a bountiful series of most signal graces; I pray thee, by the Most Holy Trinity, and by the Most Holy Names of Jesus and Mary, continually praised and invoked by thee, now that in Heaven thou enjoyest the reward of thy long penances, deign to obtain for me by thy intercession divine grace, the forgiveness of my sins, and if it so please the divine goodness, sure liberation from every travail, infirmity, grief, from every oppression and persecution of my enemies, visible and invisible; obtain for me all that is profitable to the salvation of my soul and in the end, the blessed glory of Paradise.[1]

1. Visitors to the church are encouraged to pray this prayer, displayed in Italian. The translation is by Gregory DiPippo.

CHAPTER 15: INTERIOR CHURCH AND CHAPELS

Illumination of prayer to Sant'Onofrio in Italian

O N THE RIGHT, INSIDE THE entrance, is the funerary monument of Alberto Magno Massari (1650–1712). The little statues of sainted bishops are said to be taken from an old monument to Pope Callixtus III (1378–1458) that was located in the Vatican Grottoes underneath St. Peter's Basilica (Self-Guided Tour, 11).

THE FIRST CHAPEL ON THE right is the Chapel of St. Onuphrius, dedicated to the titular patron of the church

(Self-Guided Tour, 12). This is a large rib-vaulted room that extends beyond the counter façade on the front of the church into the range adjoining the exterior arm of the loggia. The vault springs from two Doric columns on either side of the altar, creating a Gothic arch that encloses the altarpiece with a statue of St. Onuphrius—a rare sight because his image is more often than not a painted icon in the tradition of the East.

The tondo above is also attributed to Baldassarre Peruzzi, depicting God the Father. This work was done in the early sixteenth century. In addition, there are three anonymous sixteenth-century lunette frescoes depicting scenes from the life of the holy saint.

Also notable are the triangular vault panels on either side of the arch that display a pair of frescoes by an early Renaissance painter, and leading figure of the Roman school of that time, Antoniazzo degli Aquili (1430–1510), also known as Antoniazzo Romano.

One of these is easily one of the prettiest images of Our Lady in the city of Rome, an image of the Annunciation, a personal favorite of many who see it. It is believed that even the great Michelangelo himself may have come to this church to see this same work of fresco art from a century before. Our Lady is depicted kneeling in humble prayer before the angelic messenger. Her eyes are closed, while the Holy Spirit arrives in the form of a dove from Heaven. An ineffable sense of the presence of God pervades the humble daughter of Israel, the handmaiden of Nazareth. Mary, with deep reverence seen in her illumined face, reverently accedes to the fullness of God's most holy will. She is not veiled. Her hands are crossed over her

CHAPTER 15: INTERIOR CHURCH AND CHAPELS

breast. The kneeling angel, Gabriel, bears in his hands the lily, a sign of spotless purity. From a cloud above, God the Father surveys the scene.

This precious fresco is similar in style to that of Melozzo da Forlì, a contemporary who, in those days, greatly contributed to the progress of pictorial art and who occasionally assisted Antoniazzo. The genius of the image is portrayed by harmony of line and symphonic choice and arrangement of colors. Holy Mother Mary has the most beautiful face imaginable. Intense blue is predominant. As was common in the Renaissance, the background was painted as a curtain. This alone indicates the scene in Mary's house, a partial cave in Nazareth, depicted in the deep color of the night sky. In the opinion of the author, this work is a masterpiece. It harmonizes beautifully with the character of the Church, ever eager to honor God's holy will and our common mother.

❰ Detail of fresco, The Annunciation, Sant'Onofrio

PART IV: SELF-GUIDED TOUR

THE SECOND CHAPEL ON THE right-hand side of the church is the Chapel of the Madonna di Loreto (Our Lady of Loreto). This is also called the Madruzzo Chapel because the side walls have two richly decorated Baroque funerary monuments in polychrome marbles, dedicated to Cardinal Cristoforo Madruzzo and Lorenzo Madruzzo (Self-Guided Tour, 13).

The colorful lunette frescoes above the memorials date from 1605 and depict the birth of Our Lady and the Annunciation, both by Giovanni Battista Ricci (1537–1627) of the early Baroque period. The vault frescoes of the chapel are attributed to the school of Carracci, although they may also have been painted by Ricci.

The Baroque altar in this chapel has a pair of matching Corinthian columns in red-white marble, supporting a triangular pediment. The altarpiece is an oil-on-canvas painting of Our Lady resting on top of the holy house of Loreto, being carried by angels. According to the legend of Loreto, the house where Our Lady lived in Nazareth, the place attached to the cave of the Annunciation, was taken miraculously to Loreto in Italy, where it remains to this day. This painting is a characteristic Madonna of Loreto by Agostino Caracci (1557–1602), his only work kept in a church in Rome. He was the brother of the painter Annibale Caracci (1560–1609) and after the year 1580, the Carracci brothers began to develop the Baroque style of painting, focused on great drama, rich in color, and featuring extreme light and darkness.

CHAPTER 15: INTERIOR CHURCH AND CHAPELS

❧ Tomb of Archbishop Giovanni Sacco, Sant'Onofrio

T HE ARCADE ARCH ON THE RIGHT-hand side of the nave does not have a chapel; instead, a doorway leads to the sacristy (Self-Guided Tour, 15). Adjoining the sacristy entrance on the right-hand side is the tomb of Bishop Giovanni Sacco (d. 1505), Archbishop of Dubrovnik (Ragusa) in Croatia (Self-Guided Tour, 14). It is adorned with sculpture dating from the late-fifteenth and early-sixteenth centuries, the work of the school of Andrea Bregno. Above the tomb is a work of a follower of Bregno, a fifteenth-century painting of St.

Anne reading to Our Lady, framed in a rustic setting—a delightful representation of a very human exchange between the sainted mother and her most pure daughter. The moment is suffused with tenderness in the deep silence of the fields, carpeted with flowers and the brightness of the sky. All external thoughts dissipate as the mysteries of the life of Mary come into clear focus. This fresco dates from circa 1480.

LASTLY ON THE RIGHT IS THE sacristy with seventeenth-century wooden wardrobes that hold precious vestments (Self-Guided Tour, 15).

The vault is frescoed with allegorical virtues by Girolamo Pesci (1679–1759), a Baroque-style painter from Rome.

The walls have a rare Baroque-era painting of Peter of Pisa (744–799), the personal Latin tutor of the Emperor Charlemagne, by Francesco Trevisani (1656–1746). It only makes sense that an image of Peter of Pisa should be found in the sacristy as he was intended as a role model and example for clergy. As Christianity spread through Europe, so did Latin and Latinity. Peter was an expert Latinist. In the opinion of the author, in some ways, Peter might be called a patron of Latinity, or the study of Latin.

THE CHIEF INTERIOR RENAISsance decoration is seen in the elaborate apse, a colorful kaleidoscope of scenes

CHAPTER 15: INTERIOR CHURCH AND CHAPELS

from the life of Our Lady (Self-Guided Tour, 16). This touchingly beautiful wall is made up structurally of an external segmental apse, not quite semicircular, which is polygonal on the inside, with an arched ceiling conch above. Its walls are awash in a symphony of color, amid the freshness of fresco. It is a true masterpiece that involved various artists. In the image piety becomes human, the humanity of the child Jesus revealing the presence of the divine.

In the semi-circle of the apse, the famous three main panels are said to be early works of the artist Baldassarre Peruzzi (1481–1536).

In the center, *The Madonna and Child with Saints* features St. John the Baptist, St. Jerome,

❈ Apse with frescos by Baldassare Peruzzi, Sant'Onofrio

St. Catherine of Alexandria and St. Onuphrius. Below them, and kneeling off to the side, is the figure of a smaller body, that of the wealthy patron of the work. On the left, *The Nativity* portrays the Adoration of the Magi.

On the right panel is *The Escape to Egypt*. In this image, there is evident contrast between the agitation of the crowds in the Slaughter of the Innocents in the background and the serenity of the Holy Family in the fore, with movement carefully portrayed. The donkey is trotting rapidly, carrying its precious cargo, the Blessed Mother and her Divine Son, who is a little boy at this stage, while sucking his thumb, vulnerable to the profound danger at hand. St. Joseph leads from ahead, with a sack tied to a stick he carries on his shoulder, as a pilgrim on a journey.

☾ Detail of frescos by Baldassare Peruzzi, Sant'Onofrio

CHAPTER 15: INTERIOR CHURCH AND CHAPELS

BALDASSARE PERUZZI IS ALSO commonly referred to as Baldassare da Siena. Giorgio Vasari, the best-known biographer of painters, sculptors and architects from this period, writes that Peruzzi's commission to paint the chapel of the high altar in the church of Sant'Onofrio was the artist's first big commission and his first job in Rome, "which he executed in fresco with much grace and in a very beautiful manner."[2] Peruzzi's rise to fame in Rome was swift, thanks in no small part to his Roman friends and admirers as well as his works at Sant'Onofrio. "Peruzzi had come to Rome from his native Siena about 1503, and about 1504 was important among the painters working in Pinturicchio's manner at frescoing the apse wall and semi-dome of the church of S. Onofrio on the Janiculum."[3] Indeed, Peruzzi worked with his mentor Pinturicchio (1454–1513), as evidenced at San Pietro in Montorio, where they collaborated on a fresco.

After this defining project in Rome, Peruzzi developed a good repute and was summoned for more work, making him one of the most distinguished painters of his time. Vasari continues, elaborating on Peruzzi's talent, "the works which he left to us are the most honorable fruits of that true excellence which was infused in him by Heaven."[4]

Peruzzi died in Rome at age fifty-four and was buried in the Pantheon. Visitors to his grave, located next to that of Raphael (1483–1520), see his likeness along the side wall of the circular rotunda there, a carven bust in marble.

2. Giorgio Vasari, *Lives of the Painters, Sculptors and Architects*, 809.

3. S. J. Freedberg, *Painting in Italy 1500 to 1600*, 65.

4. *Ibid.*, 808.

PART IV: SELF-GUIDED TOUR

Peruzzi was not only a great painter, but also a great architect. In fact, he may truly be said never to have had an equal in his style of Renaissance architecture. Not a few art historians refer to him, in the words of Sir Reginald Blomfield, as the greatest architect of the Renaissance. Many of his sketches are studied by scholars and students of art and architecture today at the Uffizi in Florence. They attest to his phenomenal sense of spatial reasoning and his ability to design and create. The villas, palaces and churches he worked on are renowned in Rome and Siena. While Pintoricchio and Sodoma influenced him in painting, his architecture is clearly influenced by Alberti and Bramante. "Yet his style in a building or a picture, is always distinctly his own, although showing traces of his study of others' work. He never merely imitated, and this is proved by the fact that the characteristic faults of others are seldom to be found in his designs."[5]

5. William Winthrop Kent, *The Life and Works of Baldassare Peruzzi of Siena*, 11.

Peruzzi was one of the chief pre-Raphaelite painters in Rome who remained during Raphael's rise and fame. While Peruzzi's position of eminence is challenged by a great many other gifted painters of his time, in the opinion of the author, the place that he occupies is high in the history of the High Renaissance in Rome. His surviving contributions are noteworthy, if not always acknowledged. In fact, his considerable position is obscured by the unfortunate loss of a significant number of his paintings, architectural decorations and even his ephemeral scenery contributions, which were used for theatre and stage decorations and productions.

Despite the renown of Sant'Onofrio, Peruzzi is best remembered for his final architectural masterpiece, the Palazzo Massimo in Rome,

CHAPTER 15: INTERIOR CHURCH AND CHAPELS

well known for its ingenious curved front façade begun in 1535,[6] where he "reversed the normal arrangement and gave the whole facade a curve."[7] This is where St. Philip Neri himself often visited as a friend and confessor of the occupants, the Massimo family.

The images attributed to Peruzzi at Sant' Onofrio are of immense import and original talent. At the same time, they have likely been heavily retouched during previous restorations over the centuries. At the same time, he likely worked with assistants. Truth be told, we do not know exactly which images he painted. In any event, in the opinion of the author, he, himself, painted at least the three main panels on the apse wall that are attributed as his early works, as well as the fresco above entitled *The Eternal Father*. This image depicts God the Father in Heaven, raising His hand in a blessing while holding the world in His other hand. Beneath the image of the Father are the angels, who diffuse harmony with their voices and instruments in praise of all things good, true and holy. The harmony is so real it is felt, even if not heard.

6. The genius of Peruzzi the architect is made visible here where he shows off flatness against curve and hollow, small scale against larger scale, light elements against heavy, in a way that seems to mock the classical appearance of the ground story of the Palazzo Massimo.

7. Denys Hay, *The Age of the Renaissance*, 104.

❦ Detail of the Eternal Father fresco by Baldassare Peruzzi, Sant'Onofrio

These fresco paintings deserve more study and renown. They pronounce deep theological meaning, stressing the supernatural aspect of the subject depicted in the delightful style of realism, common at the time. "For the fifteenth century, the supreme object was actuality — realism."[8] The intention was to produce the most plausible and tangible impression possible, with the proviso that the images would look as realistic as possible.

In his unique style, Peruzzi reveals at times the influence of Pinturicchio (1454–1513), who painted the Borgia Apartments in the Apostolic Palace of the Vatican (today part of the Vatican Museums). The remainder of the conch frescoes are possibly by Pinturicchio. These frescoes depict in the central panel the Coronation of Our Lady, while the side panels depict apostles, saints and sibyls. The smaller five panels above depict angels playing musical instruments.

The entire wall, taken as a whole, reveals different influences and gives the impression of a garden at sunset, revealing a myriad of flowers that the fullness of the sun has already beautified. The rich images tell the story of Mary in the New Testament while showcasing the life of Christ, revealing His glory as both God and Man.

ALONG THE APSIDAL WALL OF the sanctuary is the main altar, decorated with an impressive display of polychromatic marbles that vary in color, and include yellow Siena marble around *verde antico*. The altar is dedicated to Blessed Nicola da Forca

8. Heinrich Wölfflin, *Classic Art: An Introduction to the Italian Renaissance*, 224.

CHAPTER 15: INTERIOR CHURCH AND CHAPELS

Palena (1349–1449), the priest who co-founded the Poor Hermits of St. Jerome alongside Blessed Pietro Gambacorta. Blessed Nicola's mortal remains were originally interred in the church floor. In the year 1712, these remains were exhumed and moved inside the main altar, which is shaped in the form of an elaborate sarcophagus. To this day, they remain in the altar behind a grille, flanked with two flower stems in white marble fixed on the exterior of the altar. Blessed Nicola was beatified in 1771, and the *cultus* of popular devotion has endured locally long after his passing, although it is largely forgotten today.

Tasso was originally buried in the floor of the sanctuary, near the stairs to the altar, but his remains were later moved to his first monument (Self-Guided Tour, 21) and finally moved in 1857 to the Chapel of St. Jerome (Self-Guided Tour, 20).

❬ Interior with portable altar and main high altar, Sant'Onofrio

PART IV: SELF-GUIDED TOUR

❦ Interior window in Venetian style, Sant'Onofrio

CHAPTER 15: INTERIOR CHURCH AND CHAPELS

THE THIRD CHAPEL ON THE left, closest to the sanctuary, is the Chapel of the Crucifix (Self-Guided Tour, 17). Masses for the repose of the souls of the dead have been traditionally celebrated on this altar, especially on All Souls' Day. Faithful can be seen coming here to pray for their deceased friends and family.

A marble monument to Cardinal Giuseppe Caspar Mezzofanti (1774–1849), who is reported to have spoken some thirty languages, dates from 1885 (see also Self-Guided Tour, 2). The cameo portrait and bas-relief are by Francesco Bonola (1838–1901). The monument was formerly in the adjoining chapel but was moved here in the 1950s, when the latter was refitted to honor Pope St. Pius X and the EOHSJ. In the process, the move also displaced a memorial to the marquis, Giuseppe Rondinini, (from the mid-eighteenth century), which is now kept on the outside monastery wall of the cloister atrium (Self-Guided Tour, 22).

Opposite is a memorial to Cardinal Filippo Sega (1537–1596), a papal diplomat whose titular church was Sant'Onofrio. A portrait in mosaic was done by Domenichino at the beginning of the seventeenth century.

THE SECOND CHAPEL ON THE left was originally dedicated to Blessed Peter Gambacorta (1355–1435), also

PART IV: SELF-GUIDED TOUR

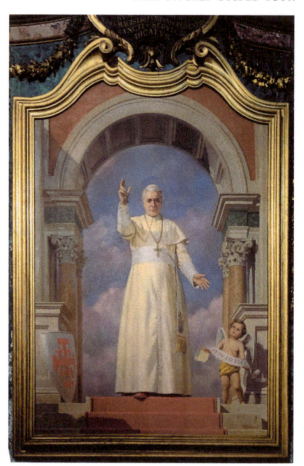

❧ Chapel of St. Pius X, Sant'Onofrio

known as Pietro da Pisa, the priest who, alongside Nicola da Forca Palena, co-founded the Poor Hermits of St. Jerome, the *Gerolomini*, who occupied the church and monastery when it was first established (Self-Guided Tour, 18). The chapel was rededicated to Pope St. Pius X, former Grand Master of the EOHSJ and the Order's only canonized saint, after he was canonized in 1954.

In a letter of May 3, 1907,[9] St. Pius X took upon himself and his successors the title of Grand Master, while delegating to the

9. *Acta Sanctae Sedis*, XL (1907), 323–24.

CHAPTER 15: INTERIOR CHURCH AND CHAPELS

Latin Patriarch, his lieutenant, the faculty to appoint in his name Knights and Dames.[10] The purpose of this action was to consolidate the position of the Order in the Holy Land and to assist in its management from Rome. In the same letter, St. Pius X also unified the design and use of uniforms and decorations for the Knights and Dames. It is he who gave the Knights the right to wear the white mantle of white wool with the red badge of the five-fold crosses attached on the left-hand side. In view of the venerable claim that the Order was a military institution, the pope also gave Knights permission to wear the jewel, the red enameled Jerusalem Cross of the Order suspended from a military trophy around the neck. In the case of the Dames, the neck emblem was to be worn hanging from a golden loop instead of as a military trophy.

The exquisite modern altarpiece, a colorful painting of St. Pius X dating from 1957, hangs above the beautiful antique altar. The altar is a superb example of *pietra dura* work, using alabaster, *verde antico* and Siena yellow marble. This very delicate style of stonework is highly precise: cutting and fitting polished colored marbles together, and assembling with great precision, with each seam fitting together seemingly perfectly. This painting replaced an earlier one by the late Baroque painter Francesco Trevisani (1656–1746), of Blessed Peter Gambacorta in prayer.

The vaulting of the ceiling and side lunettes of the chapel were restored from the earlier fresco paintings done originally by Francesco Trevisani (1656–1746). The same artist painted the frescoes both on the cupola vault and on

10. The office of Grand Master continued to be vested in the person of the Holy Father until 1928, when the decree was later updated by Pope Pius XI, who appointed the Patriarch of Jerusalem as *Rector and Perpetual Administrator*.

◖ Tomb of Cardinal Canali, Sant'Onofrio

the pendentives, the four triangular segments that bear the weight of the dome. Meanwhile, in the lunettes, his frescoes depicting scenes from the life of Blessed Peter Gambacorta have unfortunately since been covered over.

Along the wall is a neoclassical funeral memorial to Cardinal Nicola Canali (1874–1961), placed here in 1969. Canali, born into a noble family of marquises in Rieti, was ordained priest in the Holy Year 1900 and created cardinal in 1935. He was a member not only of the EOHSJ, but also of the Sovereign Military Order of Malta. During his distinguished career at the service of the Vatican, he held many important roles, including Grand Master of the EOHSJ, which he was appointed in 1949. Previous to this appointment, he had been appointed Protector of the Order in 1940. He is often seen in period photos of papal liturgies standing next to the pope in his role as first deacon (*Primo Diacono*) of the College of Cardinals. His motto was *Semper Fidelis* (Always Faithful).

THE FIRST CHAPEL ON THE LEFT, closest to the entrance, is the Chapel of St. Jerome (Self-Guided Tour, 19). This chapel is twice as deep as the two other chapels on the left-hand side of the church. In its vaulting, it boasts two cupolas—a rare sight, even in Rome.

By order of Pope Blessed Pius IX (1792–1878), in 1857, Carlo Piccoli fitted the chapel to accommodate a large, second memorial to the famous Renaissance poet Torquato Tasso, seen on the right (Self-Guided Tour, 20). The altar is properly oriented East.

The altarpiece, a painting of St. Jerome in Bethlehem, is by the painter Filippo Balbi (1806–1890), who also frescoed the two cupolas. The cupola closest to the entrance depicts God the Father, while the other, located over the altar, depicts red, white and gold scrollwork paneling, with the oculus depicting a fresco of the Apotheosis of St. Jerome, rising on a cloud guided up to Heaven. The heraldry in the pendentives is of Pope Blessed Pius IX, who in 1847 reinstated the Latin Patriarch (residential bishop with all its privileges) in Jerusalem and reserved to him the exclusive right to create knights. In 1868, Pope Blessed Pius IX also gave the Order a revised constitution, defining thus a new period of its history.

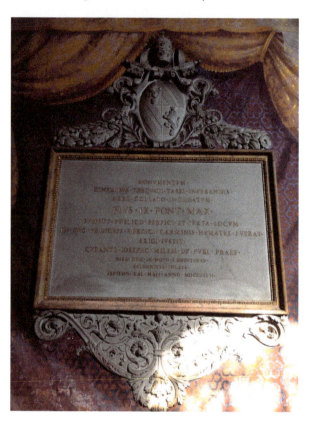

◖ Plaque from reign of Blessed Pius IX, Sant'Onofrio

Two bronze busts are found on the side walls. The first depicts the painter Bernardo Celentano (1835–1863), who died in Rome and was buried in the Church of Sant'Onofrio. One of his major works was a painting entitled *Tasso, Starting to Show Madness at Bisaccia*. The other is of the sculptor Giuseppe De Fabris (1790–1860), the artist responsible for the second Tasso monument (Self-Guided Tour, 20).

CHAPTER 15: INTERIOR CHURCH AND CHAPELS

❦ Bust in memory of a painter artist, Sant'Onofrio

O**N THE RIGHT OF THE CHAPEL,** the magnificent neoclassical tomb of Torquato Tasso, the second and larger of the monuments to him, draws curious crowds and student groups. Tasso was originally buried in the floor of the sanctuary of near the stairs to

117

the altar (Self-Guided Tour, 16). Partly because he himself on his deathbed had requested a simple and modest tomb, the first monument planned by his close friend Cardinal Cinzio Aldobrandini (Self-Guided Tour, 21) took several years to materialize.

Tasso's remains were moved to the chapel in 1857 when Giuseppe De Fabris (1790–1860) of Vicenza, a follower of the famous sculptor Antonio Canova (1757–1822), completed this work, which many describe as technically accomplished, feeding the soul with beauty and order. At the time, the new tomb in tribute to the poet's supreme artistic achievements was harshly criticized by some, who disagreed over what type of tomb would be most fitting.

Its form is an arched niche in marble, at the base of which is a relief depicting Tasso's crowded funeral procession through the streets of Rome. The statue, shows the poet directing his gaze up to the Heavens for inspiration as he writes, looking up at Our Lady in prayer. He is also depicted leaning on a shield carved with the words *Pro Fide*, referring to St. Paul's advice to Christians that the only sure weapon is prayer and holiness. "In all things taking the shield of faith, wherewith you may be able to extinguish all the fiery darts of the most wicked one" (Ephesians 6:16 Douay–Rheims). Behind the shield is a military trophy, evoking in some ways the insignia of the Knights of the Holy Sepulchre.

Buried in the same tomb with Tasso is Francesco Patrizi (1529–1597), a colleague of his who was a philosopher and scientist from Venice, of Dalmatian (Croatian) descent (see Self-Guided Tour, 2). Some Italian students of

CHAPTER 15: INTERIOR CHURCH AND CHAPELS

❦ The tomb of Torquato Tasso, Sant'Onofrio

literature and history also study Patrizi's works in Italian and Latin, as he was one of the last Renaissance humanists. As a young man he had sailed the Mediterranean with his uncle, the commander of a galley, in defense against the Ottoman Turks.

The lunette on the wall opposite the Tasso monument depicts the poet on his deathbed.

119

PART IV: SELF-GUIDED TOUR

On the left of the main entrance of the church is this first modest monument to Torquato Tasso, with a painted portrait of the poet (Self-Guided Tour, 21). From their original burial place in the sanctuary of the church (Self-Guided Tour, 16), his remains were transferred and kept here until 1857, when they were moved to the present tomb (Self-Guided Tour, 20).

The Marquis of Villa, one of Tasso's many close friends, visited Sant'Onofrio five years after the poet's death, only to find no proper tomb had yet been constructed. He earnestly entreated permission from Cardinal Cinzio Aldobrandini to build a tomb in Tasso's memory. All that he could obtain was permission to erect a temporary marble tablet with a brief inscription to be placed by the monks over Tasso's ashes. Eight more years passed without any action, whereupon another of Tasso's dearest friends, Cardinal Bonifazio Bevilacqua Aldobrandini (1571–1627), uncle of Pope Gregory XIV and a great patron of the arts, took it upon himself to raise on the left of the entrance this elegant and stately monument. It was completed in 1544, nearly fifteen years after Tasso's passing.

The inscription, translated from the most suitable of poetic languages, Latin, reads thus:

> (The resting place or monument)
> of the poet Torquato Tasso.
>
> Ah, how much renown and
> praise are in this one name!

CHAPTER 15: INTERIOR CHURCH AND CHAPELS

❦ The second tomb of Torquato Tasso, Sant'Onofrio

Boniface Cardinal Bevilacqua translated his bones and laid them to rest here, lest the remains of one who lives as he is constant spoken of by men be honored and sought out in a place too little splendid. The love of virtue urged (him to do this), religious duty urged (him) as a fellow citizen and a friend of his family. He lived for 51 years, born in a great, most flourishing and good age, in the year 1544.

He shall live, we are not deceived, forever, in the memory, admiration and honor of men.[11]

11. Translation by Gregory DiPippo.

16
The Renaissance Cloister

HE ATRIUM ACTS AS a covered tunnel connecting the outside (Self-Guided Tour, 6) to the monastery entrance as well as the interior cloister (Self-Guided Tour, 23)—an outdoor courtyard not to be missed.

❦ Outside entrance to cloister, Sant'Onofrio

Inside the connecting vestibule are funerary monuments that were displaced from the interior of the church during renovations in 1957 (Self-Guided Tour, 22). Dating from 1801, a neo-Baroque skeleton in a shroud commemorates a Roman art collector, the Marquis Giuseppe Rondinini (1725–1801). There is also a monument to the dramatist and poet Alessandro Guidi (1650–1721).

A plaque commemorates the work done on the property by Venerable Pius XII. This was completed in 1947, after the property was given over to the EOHSJ:

PART IV: SELF-GUIDED TOUR

❦ Outside plaque commemorating renovation under the pontificate of Venerable Pius XII, Sant'Onofrio

HAS AEDES RELIGIONI INGENVISQVE
ARTIBVS SACRAS
QVAE EXTREMOS TORQVATI TASSI
RECREARVNT DIES

PIVS X̄Ī̄Ī PONT MAX

EQVESTRI ORDINI A S SEPVLCRO HIEROSOL
CONCREDIDIT
IDEMQVE ORDO AERE PROPRIO RESTAVRAVIT
A M̄D̄C̄C̄C̄C̄X̄X̄X̄X̄V̄ĪĪ

Pope Pius XII entrusted these buildings, sacred to religion and the liberal arts, which refreshed the last days of Torquato Tasso, to the Equestrian Order of the Holy Sepulchre of Jerusalem, and the same Order restored them at its own expense in the year 1947.[1]

1. Translation by Gregory DiPippo.

☩

THE PLEASANT LITTLE INNER cloister adjoining the west side of the church attracts many visitors, including students of art, architecture, and engineering and design who come to study or sketch or just admire the cloister area (Self-Guided Tour, 23). Such a refreshing work of the Renaissance period to observe from the mid-fifteenth century! It is one of the quietest and most secluded havens in the venerable city, with beautiful potted flowers and ivy drooping from the ledges, a charming

CHAPTER 16: THE RENAISSANCE CLOISTER

place to visit, especially, in the opinion of the author, during a rainfall. The nineteenth-century French writer Stendhal visited the cloister in 1815, purportedly declaring it quite poetically as the most beautiful place to die.

❦ The inner cloister, Sant'Onofrio

The two-story cloister is rectangular with arcades on all four sides on the main level, with ancient columns taken from different buildings of ancient Rome crowned with Renaissance capitals. The second story is an upper arcade gallery that is a horizontal entablature, supported by Renaissance brick columns that are uniquely octagonal, dating from the time of construction. The section of the main level floor that is covered is tiled while the outside floor is cobbled.

The columns on the main level are made of various stones, including eight in cipollino marble, three in grey granite, two in *marmo tasio* (a rare white marble from a Greek island), two in grey marble, one in red granite from Egypt, and four in *marmo imezio* (believed to be from Turkey). Two of the oldest columns are worth mentioning. The fifth column on the long side on the left is believed to be of the period between the fifth and sixth centuries AD while the second to last column on the long side on the right is said to be from the Imperial Period of ancient Rome.

❧ The inner cloister, Sant'Onofrio

The cloister's outdoor lunette frescoes on the walls have survived damp winters and hot summers ever since they were completed to celebrate the Holy Year 1600, with restorations performed in 1682. They depict stories of the life and legend of St. Onuphrius, each with a caption in Latin and an Italian translation. From the entrance on the right are the first four, attributed to the Mannerist painter Giuseppe Cesari (1568–1640), also known as *Cavalier d'Arpino* (a title he acquired after he was knighted by his patron, Clement VIII). The remaining frescoes are attributed to Sebastiano Strada and Claudio Ridolfi (1560–1644), who were of his school. These images each have a caption, describing in some detail the life and legend of the saint.

17
Monastery Upper Floor: The Museum and Madonna

THE TASSO MUSEUM, known as the Museo Tassiano, is housed in a few rooms in the upper floor of the old monastery, including the room where the poet died (Self-Guided Tour, 24). Visits to the museum are by appointment only. Through the centuries the monks maintained this attraction as a visitor center for the fans of Tasso and his poetry. In 1930, ownership of the contents of the museum was passed to the Holy See. The present version of the museum was assembled and inaugurated in 1939.

❧ Tasso Museum, the room where the poet died, Sant'Onofrio convent

Tasso's museum, although small, preserves some interesting items of historical value — made all the more important because, for students and visitors, Tasso is a crucial link between the fading classical and medieval culture with the

PART IV: SELF-GUIDED TOUR

new Christian culture of the Renaissance. The museum includes various personal memorabilia, including a crucifix he held as he died. One of the main items of interest is his original funeral mask, a wax effigy made just after he passed. In addition, one can see the box that once contained his remains when he was first interred in the church. Lastly, a collection of early editions of Tasso's works can be seen along with samples of his letters and unique handwriting.

☩

❦ Madonna and Child with Donor fresco, Sant'Onofrio convent

On the second floor of the convent, at the entrance to the apartment of Tasso, is another artistic treasure not to be missed (Self-Guided Tour, 24). This hidden gem is a bonus treat to all who visit the museum: a fresco of the Madonna with Child, together with a figure of the artist's patron, a forgotten man holding his cap while the Christ Child reaches out to bless him. This image has now been admired for centuries and is called *The*

CHAPTER 17: MONASTERY UPPER FLOOR: THE MUSEUM AND MADONNA

Madonna and Child with Donor. The figure of the wealthy patron of the work stands out, with the stupendous profile of a nobleman—while definitely not a monk, his identity has been lost to history.

Originally, the work was surrounded by a precious Renaissance frame of maiolica, a beautiful tin-glazed pottery decorated in colors on a white background. This is a rare sight in Rome, while much more common in Florence. The frame is said to have been the work of a disciple of Giovanni della Robbia, a famous ceramic artist of the Italian Renaissance.

In former generations the fresco was attributed to Leonardo da Vinci, even though this has always been called into question. While the image has understandably aged in places and the colors have slightly altered with the passage of time, the sublime touch of the influence of da Vinci is clear. For example, the figures in the image resemble very much his visual style, structured in the *pyramid* construction so common with the master and obvious in his previous works of the same period. This includes the mysterious evanescent coloring of so many of his figures, showing characteristic shadings that are seen in his previous works, and revealing simple tones in contrast with more vivid colors. Even though in past generations, many have attributed the fresco to da Vinci himself, current authorities are content that the artist was instead most likely a member of his school. This is an obvious explanation for the similarity of style, as it was common enough in those years for the design and stylistic features of da Vinci to have been borrowed and copied. The work has also often been attributed to Giovanni

Antonio Boltraffio (1466–1516), who worked in the studio of da Vinci. Others have attributed it to Cesare da Sesto (1477–1523), who was one of the *Leonardeschi,* a large group of artists who worked in the studio of (or under the influence of) da Vinci. It could be that da Sesto painted the lunette while he was purportedly working with Peruzzi in the year 1505.

It is the opinion of the author that the artist of this work is most likely Cesare da Sesto. While other artists are more affected and more scholastic in their approach, da Sesto has a demonstrated ability to depict the sublime indeterminateness and value of line that is so eminently the mark of da Vinci and his students, under the inspiration of his influential Tuscan style. Regardless of authorship, the painting remains one of the most delightful pictorial depictions of the mother and child to be seen in Rome.

18
Conclusion

T.S. ELIOT, IN HIS POEM *The Waste Land*, describes the modern city as a soulless desert. Not so with Christian Rome. Rome, more than any other city in the world, is a city of churches. It is this aspect that first strikes the visitor, especially North Americans. The pilgrim is immediately struck by the juxtaposition of the worldliness and glamour of the city, the sheer number and grandeur of the churches and the opulent display of art. The fascination lies in the spectacle the city offers thanks to its extraordinary vocation.

The artistic debris of centuries and the accretions of beautiful and pleasing works of art trace the footsteps of generations seeking the infinite, ordinary people looking for God. Indeed, the art speaks a language in response to the cravings of the human soul. Thus, the road is paved for the pilgrim who arrives at Rome, the portal to another world. Every pilot looks to the sky for direction. While many moderns are indifferent, pilgrims are led to Sant'Onofrio with their eyes upwards. They are led to a church still resplendent with the atmosphere of the Renaissance. Pilgrims journey and stand inside the porch of a church where countless others have experienced the same journey and arrival.

Meanwhile, in the moral influence that a chosen city can exercise on artistic genius, Rome is supreme. Rome has been called the common birthplace of every child of Western civilization. As it is said, all roads lead to Rome. It has been repeated many times that there is no great act, no great man, whose beginning or end was not in Rome. For this reason many have wished to be buried anywhere in the city, the cradle of Western civilization, while close to the tomb of the Blessed Apostle Peter in the Vatican. Rome has molded the nations and peoples of the world. She it is who has breathed her spirit into the soul of Europe and has been the central hearth-flame of the West.

The daily life of all is permeated with the life and history of the city. Meanwhile, Sant'Onofrio overlooks the city as a citadel of faith. Not only pilgrims and tourists arrive at the gates of Sant'Onofrio, but also artists worthy of the name, poets who aspire to understand and create, historians who desire to know. Not to mention, young people who feel themselves capable of attaining a high degree of culture and spiritual awareness while coming into contact with the message of Sant'Onofrio.

This little work on the history, art and personages of Sant'Onofrio came into being from personal visits to the church and standing in the very place where history was made. The authentic sense of the beauty, the history and faith of the people who have come before has inspired the author to capture their story. In addition, attending Holy Mass at this altar and seeing vested Knights and Dames processing in and out amid the echo of the Gregorian melodies chanted in Latin and reverberating through the vaults above has inspired the author to make this little contribution, especially to pilgrim members of the Equestrian Order.

Beauty pleases the visitor and demands to be noticed at Sant'Onofrio. It speaks to the pilgrim directly, like the voice of an old friend. With an enrapturing appeal, it demands wonder and reverence, and fills the visitor who is touched by grace with an untroubled and consoling delight. It reveals itself as a real and universal value, an invocatory presence, anchored in objective principles of taste and the rational nature of the human intellect and will. Thus the Catholic experience at Sant'Onofrio is fundamentally an encounter with beauty: a real and true sense of beauty is unleashed to play an indispensable role in shaping the experience of the visitor. Beauty and the sacred are deeply connected in our human emotions. According to Plato and Plotinus, beauty is an ultimate value, something that is pursued for its own sake. Beauty, truth and goodness are a trio: three ultimate values that speak to the soul and reveal the Creator and His relationship to us. The experience of beauty is therefore compared similarly to that of truth and goodness, ways in which divine unity and goodness are made known to the human soul. St. Thomas Aquinas regarded truth, goodness and unity as *transcendentals*: features of reality, aspects of being. Poets, philosophers and theologians who visit Sant'Onofrio point towards beauty in its highest form, to God the metaphysical source of all beauty.

In sharp contrast to modern churches of today that are understood primarily in terms of their utility, Sant'Onofrio is a sound piece of good art that ravishes the beholder and listener by a secret harmony of proportions and acoustics. While modern philosophy explains modern art, Catholic philosophy explains Renaissance church art. In the words of Archbishop Fulton Sheen: "Art is the lyrical expression of philosophy."[1]

1. Fulton Sheen, *Old Errors and New Labels*, 77.

This is why in the Renaissance they painted and sculpted and built a certain way. It reflects how the people thought and prayed and created and found a spiritual home. Meanwhile, in the words of Sir Roger Scruton, "The classical templates affirm what is sempiternal in the midst of change, and tell us that we belong where we are, and belong as a community."[2]

2. Roger Scruton, *The Aesthetics of Architecture*, xi.

As the temple informs the city, Sant'Onofrio calls and beckons through its sacred history with a message for all. Just as a living faith must change and transform the life of a believer, so a religion must influence and transform the social way of life, the culture. It is the hope of the author that precisely the sacred beauty of Sant'Onofrio will be its message that is projected and received by the earnest pilgrim who goes in honest search. The message of Sant'Onofiro is one of not only beauty, but also grandeur, permanence and tradition. A testimony of faith, hope, and charity. It is a center of worship, contemplation and community. As the history of spirituality indicates, "There is something intrinsically beautiful about the domain of the sacred. It draws us to itself in a different way than other beautiful objects, and when we appreciate it (contemplate it), it pleases, fulfills, and enchants us, and most importantly, it brings us into the very heart of divine beauty — into the heart of God."[3]

3. Robert Spitzer, S. J., *Finding True Happiness*, 133.

Finally, Sant' Onofrio is a symbol of life removed from the world of decay and dissolution, hiding in its inner sanctum a divine apartness. Sacred things have always been removed, held apart and preserved through the ages, specifically because of their important role of placing the transcendental subject before the eyes of the

Chapter 18: Conclusion

visitor and within grasp. Roman churches have long been considered a preamble to the city of Heaven and for this reason they are generally as beautiful as possible, visible and well maintained. Visitors to Rome learn from tour guides that pilgrimage is a metaphor for life and that all people are on a journey to God: everyone is a pilgrim. In Rome, the pilgrim meets a city that is old and in decay... and learns that it has always been this way. Such is the course of an ancient and noble city, the Eternal City, which waits for all pilgrims, past, present and future.

Nevertheless Sant'Onofrio, in its hidden location and current state, awaits new life. While much of Sant'Onofrio has been aged and damaged by time and damp neglect, in a spirit of true pragmatism, let us hope and pray for new life for this venerable treasure, a true citadel of faith, a good way and a path forever preserved for future generations to find refreshment: "Thus saith the Lord: Stand ye on the ways, and see and ask for the old paths which is the good way, and walk ye in it: and you shall find refreshment for your souls" (Jeremias 6:16 Douay–Rheims).

BIBLIOGRAPHY

Acta Sanctae Sedis, XL (1907). Vatican City: Tipographia Vaticana, 1907.

Anderson, Robin. *Rome Churches of Special Interest for English-Speaking People*. Vatican City: Libreria Editrice Vaticana, 1982.

Attwater, Donald. *A Catholic Dictionary*. New York: Macmillan, 1958.

Beny, Roloff and Peter Gunn. *The Churches of Rome*. New York: Simon and Schuster, 1981.

Blasco, Sir Alfred J. *The Modern Crusaders*. New Jersey: Pen Rose, 1998.

Cross, Milton and David Ewen. *Encyclopedia of the Great Composers and Their Music*. Volume I. Garden City, New York: Doubleday, 1953.

D'Arezzo, Leonardo Bruni. *De Studiis et Literis*, translated by W.H. Woodward. Cambridge: Cambridge University Press, 1912.

D'Assemani, Michael H. Abraham. *The Cross on the Sword*. Chicago: Photopress, 1944.

Dawson, Christopher. *Christianity and European Culture*. Washington, D.C.: The Catholic University of America Press, 1998.

— *The Dividing of Christendom*. San Francisco: Ignatius Press, 2008.

— *The Formation of Christendom*. San Francisco: Ignatius Press, 2008.

Digby, Henry Kenelm. *The Broad Stone of Honour: Or the True Sense and Practice of Chivalry. Tancredus*. London: Edward Lumley, Chancery Land, 1846.

Durant, Will. *The Story of Civilization*. New York: Simon & Schuster, 1950.

Folsom, Frank. *Saint Onofrio on the Janiculum*. Special Edition Printed Occasional Papers, Volume II, 1961.

Forgeng, Jeffry and Will McLean. *Daily Life in Chaucer's England*. Westport, Connecticut: Greenwood, 2008.

Freedberg, S.J. *Painting in Italy 1500 to 1600*. Middlesex, England: Penguin, 1970.

Hay, Denys. *The Age of the Renaissance*. New York: McGraw-Hill, 1967.

Kent, William Winthrop. *The Life and Works of Baldassare Peruzzi of Siena*. New York: Architectural Book Publishing, 1925.

Liturgical Conference. *Mary in the Liturgy*. Elsberry, Mo., 1955.

Messori, Vittorio. *The Ratzinger Report: An Exclusive Interview on the State of the Church*. San Francisco: Ignatius Press, 1985.

Newman, John Henry, *Essays Critical and Historical*. London: Longmans, Green, and Co., 1919.

O'Connell, Canon J.B., ed. *The Roman Martyrology*. Westminster, Maryland: The Newman Press, 1962.

Regnault, Lucien. *The Day-to-Day Life of the Desert Fathers in Fourth-Century Egypt*. St. Bede's Press, 2002.

Russell, Norman. *The Lives of the Desert Fathers*. Collegeville: Cistercian Publications, 1981.

Scruton, Roger. *The Aesthetics of Architecture*. Princeton: Princeton University Press, 2013.

— *Beauty: A Very Short Introduction*. Oxford: Oxford University Press, 2011.

Sheen, Fulton. *Old Errors and New Labels*. New York: St. Paul's/Alba House, 2007.

Spitzer, Robert. *Finding True Happiness: Satisfying Our Restless Hearts*. San Francisco: Ignatius Press, 2015.

Van der Veldt, James. *The Ecclesiastical Orders of Knighthood*. Washington, DC: Catholic University Press, 1956.

van Zeller, Hubert. *The Holy Rule: Notes on St. Benedict's Legislation for Monks*. New York: Sheed and Ward, 1958.

Vasari, Giorgio. *Lives of the Painters, Sculptors and Architects*, Volume I. New York: Alfred A. Knopf, 1996.

Vivian, Tim. *Paphnutius: Histories of the Monks of Upper Egypt and the Life of Onnophrius*. Collegeville: Cistercian Publications, 2000.

Ward, Wilfrid Philip. *The Life of John Henry Cardinal Newman*. Volume I. London: Longmans, Green & Co., 1912.

Wiffen, J. H. *The Jerusalem Delivered: A Life of the Author* (with *The Life of Tasso* supplement). London, Covent Garden: Henry G. Bohn, 1854.

Wölfflin, Heinrich. *Classic Art: An Introduction to the Italian Renaissance*. London: The Phaidon Press, 1953.

ABOUT THE AUTHOR

JOHN PAUL SONNEN IS FOUNDER and principal of Orbis Catholic Travel LLC. He is one of six children and the product of Catholic education. In 2001, he graduated from the University of St. Thomas in St. Paul, Minnesota with a degree in Catholic Studies. That same year, he moved to Vladivostok, Russia, to volunteer as a lay missioner. In 2004, at age twenty-four, he moved to Rome to pursue graduate studies at the Pontifical University of St. Thomas Aquinas, where he earned his graduate degrees in the dogma section of the Faculty of Theology. In 2011, he married Natalie Hudson of Vancouver, British Columbia. They welcomed their first child in 2012. Since 2014, he has been a Knight of the Order of the Holy Sepulchre and also a Knight of the Sovereign Military Order of Malta, both honors in recognition of his services to the Church and works of charity on two continents. In his free time, John Paul enjoys his family, garden, library, photography, and visiting churches and museums. His favorite subject is history, and his preferred travel destinations include Rome and Jerusalem.

ACKNOWLEDGMENTS

GRATEFUL ACKNOWLEDGMENT is due to Dr. Evan Michael Mary Simpkins of California, a Thomas Aquinas College graduate and Aristotelian philosopher, who benignantly introduced me to the glories of Tasso when he guided me up to Tasso's oak on the Janiculum in March 2010, an event that so inspired me I wrote an ode:

> Sant'Onofrio enters into your world, you find it there.
> Tasso is my poem then, forever in my heart
> More beautiful than a sonnet, you made rhyme
> And I had received you unaware.

Further acknowledgment is due to Sir Amer Shehadeh, KCHS, teacher, guide, and friend from Nazareth, whose influence in the field of faith-based tourism in the Holy Land during his service of more than thirty years as a local Christian guide has been felt worldwide. I am forever indebted to him for showing my brother and me around Jerusalem in May 2017.

Also to Sir Bao Dang, KHS, who has accompanied me on a great many travel adventures to Rome, including a most memorable visit in May 2015 to the newly opened Hotel Gran Meliá Rome on the Janiculum Hill (Villa Agrippina), with fond memories of seeing Sant'Onofrio from the hotel windows.

Finally, immense gratitude is due to Alan Yoshioka and the reposed Theresa Yoshioka, whom I first met in Toronto in 2011. Together they encouraged me to lead my first pilgrimage

SANT'ONOFRIO AL GIANICOLO

tour, and Alan's masterful editing has brought order to my sprawling recollections of the magnificent site that is the subject of this volume.

CPSIA information can be obtained
at www.ICGtesting.com
Printed in the USA
LVHW071508120723
751942LV00075B/215/J